The Basic Guide to
Selling Arts & Crafts

James Dillehay

Warm Snow Publishers
Torreon, New Mexico

Published by:
Warm Snow Publishers
P.O. Box 75
Torreon, NM 87061
505-384-1102

Cover design by Janet Norquist

ISBN: 0-9629923-0-5
Library of Congress Cat. Card No.: 93-061279

Printed and bound in the United States of America

Printed on recycled, acid-free papers ∞

Library Systems and Services Cataloging in Publication Data

Dillehay, James.
    The basic guide to selling arts & crafts / James Dillehay. -- 1st ed.
    p.   cm.
    Includes bibliographical references and index.
    ISBN 0-9629923-0-5
    1. Handicraft--Marketing. I. Title. II. Title: Selling arts & crafts.
III. Title: Selling arts and crafts.

HF5439.H27D54 1994   745.5'068'1--dc20   93-61279

Table of Contents

List of Tables and Illustrations

Introduction

Hundreds of overlooked opportunities for selling arts and crafts products exist for both beginning and experienced craftspersons. *The Basic Guide to Selling Arts & Crafts* gives you cost effective success tips in simple, step-by-step guidelines. You'll learn how to recognize which products sell best, where to locate buyers, how much to charge for your work to earn the maximum profit, what it takes to sell to stores, galleries, interior designers, and much more.

This book takes the artist and craftsperson through the basics of beginning sales all the way to selling at trade shows and to corporations. The information is in these pages; all you have to do is decide how large you want your business to grow. You can keep the business a simple one-person shop or hire others to help produce and sell your wares. Many of the ideas here will work well for either part or full-time income. *The Basic Guide* will help you evaluate your business desires and show you how to reach your goals. The best news is you can start from home right now for little start-up costs.

Learn how to sell your first pieces to friends and relatives without high pressure sales techniques and have fun at the same time. Later, when you have acquired a large enough inventory, Chapter 3 will give you everything you need to know to enter and succeed at art and craft shows. Chapters 4 and 5 help you learn what it takes to sell to stores and trade shows.

Is your craftwork suitable for a mail order business? Chapter 7 tells you insider tips and how to make it work. Have you thought about the lucrative interior design market for your arts and crafts? Turn to Chapter 6 for important advice.

You can have great sales from all your ideas, but if you don't know how much profit you're actually clearing, you could be working for less than minimum wage. Check Chapters 2, 9 and 10 for how to keep records, price your work and plan your business for maximum profits.

If you think you've done everything you could to sell your work and it still doesn't move, don't give up until you've seen the important solutions offered in Chapter 12, What To Do If Your Work Isn't Selling.

Expand beyond making and selling arts and crafts into one or more of the spin-off business ideas that are all based on your craft experiences. The Appendixes list hundreds of resources of organizations, magazines about crafts, booth suppliers, craft show guides, trade show producers, craft schools, and much more.

The information and guidance found in this book come from my years of making and selling handwoven garments, accessories, rugs, and fiber art; experiences and stories of other craftspersons I have met along the way; and several years as the vice-president of a chain of retail stores in Texas. I have included both success stories and failures, too, to help save you time and money from making similar mistakes.

My hope is that the ideas you find here will help you accomplish these four things: 1) inspire you to plan your own destiny, 2) help you gain the financial independence that gives you time to create great masterpieces, 3) become the richest person on your block, and 4) take enough time to spend the night with your spouse occasionally (best of luck on that one).

There's plenty of tips in these pages on all aspects of starting and expanding your art or craft business, but I've found three things that play a bigger role in achieving success than any other — patience, persistence, and positive attitude. If you learn and cultivate these traits, you will always survive even when things look their worst.

If you are the kind of person who seeks perfection in creating your art, the buying public will reward you. Customers will tell you a lot about your work, but be aware, success will come from paying attention to what they buy.

Chapter 1
Finding Buyers

My first craft piece was a woven sampler scarf using many different patterns, yarns, and colors. I had just cut the piece off the loom when a friend walked by. All I wanted to do was wrap it around my bench and use it as a cushion. But he complimented it, saying *"No, you should sell it, someone will love this."* I wasn't so sure. Another friend, Janet, visiting the area from New York, walked by my loom the next day and saw the scarf where I had draped it over the castle. She fell in love with the piece and told me she wanted to buy it.

Since I was new to crafts, I had no idea how much to charge. Meekly, I said *"How about $20."* She said okay, and that was how my business started. Later, Janet asked me to make her a shawl, then another scarf, then later a few for gifts. Her boyfriend, Tom, seeing my work, ordered something special for her. The next few months continued like that, bringing a series of orders from friends, learning experiences, and a growing inventory of pieces to sell.

The simplest way to begin selling is to start making things. When friends and relatives see the products you make, they'll be the first to want them. The more you make, the more you will sell. You have probably experienced some of these easy sales already.

Door-to-door sales

You may think door-to-door selling is only for ency-clopedias and vacuum cleaners, not art or craftwork. I know of two persons, however, who did quite well with this method. One gentleman approached my booth at a craft show. Seeing my woven pieces, reminded him of his own experiences. His mother had been a weaver and had taught him and later his children, how to weave rag rugs. She encouraged them to sell the pieces in the neighborhood by going door-to-door and taking orders from a variety of samples. The neighbors were so impressed with the young weaver's enterprising they often bought rugs and told other friends. The kids did the weaving and the selling after school and made their own spending money from the business.

Another friend of mine related how she used to go door-to-door in her neighborhood with a selection of homemade potholders. After she noted the colors used in each neighbor's kitchen, she went home and custom made potholders to match the existing color schemes. The neighbor's were so impressed, she sold several dozen just on her nearby blocks.

This kind of business can work with a variety of craft items for the home like rag rugs, placemats, cross-stitch and needlepoint pillows, woven throws, and quilts. Once the customer knows you, the door is open to selling them additional pieces, possibly even other personal items like handmade earrings, necklaces and bracelets. The only cost of making door-to-door sales is your time and effort.

Making craft products suitable for home sales is an easy and inexpensive source of income. For example, the cost of materials for making rag rugs and placemats comes to almost nothing. I found thrift stores willing to sell huge bags of clothing unsuitable for resale for only a few dollars. There are also companies who advertise in the craft magazines, like *Handwoven,* that sell rag material pre-cut in one or two inch widths on tubes that can save you cutting the rags yourself.

When selling door-to-door, make up a set of samples of everything you produce. Type up an order form and price list of custom sizes, photocopy it, and then go out and take orders. Such a business is a perfect starting place for a part or full-time income.

The only obstacle for most is the knocking on doors. You must be the kind of individual who isn't discouraged by rejections. The great thing is, though, it doesn't cost anything to try. This is also a way of building a base of customers who might later want to sponsor home parties.

Home parties (boutiques)

When I sent some of my first craftwork as Christmas gifts to my sister and mother, they liked them so much they set up a home party and invited many of their friends. Easy sales like these in a comfortable atmosphere will quickly boost your enthusiasm for getting your business going. A home party is not only fun, one can be arranged quickly and inexpensively. A friend that's seen and bought your work will often be willing to host an evening or afternoon party, especially if you offer a commission of 10 to 15% of the sales.

The best season for a home show is the month before Christmas, as this is the hottest selling period of the year. Usually, a home party is convenient between seven and ten in the evening. Invite as many persons as your host is comfortable with. Send out personal invitation cards announcing the event. Local newspapers might even list it in their calender of events. Send them a news release to let them know the details. See page 99 for more on publicity.

Offer refreshments and create an informal, party atmosphere. At some point, give a brief talk or demonstration about your art or craft. The more you know and can talk about what you do, the more value the listeners will put on the products. It's also easy for the listener to get excited about buying something you have made.

To avoid awkwardness, make it clear after you have talked about your craft that anyone interested can purchase items then. It is better for you to have someone buying pieces at this time than to take orders. Once someone has paid for something, they are less inclined to change their mind about it later. Acquaintances may take familiarity as an invitation to open a charge account with you. Unless you want to deal with the hassles of collecting bills, ask for payment with the sale.

Because production costs of a home show are low, you might discount your normal prices as an incentive for persons to come. Consider giving away one or two pieces as a door prize. Also, announce that anyone being a host to a party for you in the future will receive a commission. I found, though, my sponsors usually wanted to take their percentage in merchandise. This is great, because when you give them the retail value of your products, you have only spent as much as it cost you to make the item.

If you like these events, you could expand into larger productions. You might, through your home party contacts, seek sponsoring by a local organization in return for a commission on the sales. Invite a few other craftspersons to show their work and charge a fee or percentage of their sales. Maybe you have a friend with a complementary craft. For example if you make clothing items, another craftsperson offers handbags, and someone else sells jewelry.

These events could become popular enough that you have to find a larger location and rent selling spaces to more vendors. This grows into its own business after awhile and you might find yourself spending more time organizing shows than making your craft. See Chapter 13, for more on becoming a show producer.

Craft cooperatives (co-ops)

If you like working with others, consider joining a cooperative gallery with other artists and craftspersons. Cooperatives require little investment from you and provide an excellent way to test your products and display ideas. There are many operations like this across the country. Almost all of them have a jury process similar to the art and craft shows that will be explained fully in Chapter 3. Call or visit one to find out how they interview new artists.

Every cooperative gallery has its own rules of operating. In some, you will be required to work at the gallery a certain number of hours per month and pay monthly dues. Others charge a monthly rental fee and hire sales help and bookkeepers to operate the business. In either case, you usually pay a percentage of the retail sales to the gallery at the time a sale is made.

Some of my best sales have come through galleries that were jointly owned by several artists. Usually when other artists are involved in the running of a gallery, their support for you as an artisan will be more helpful. Also, working at the gallery provides the advantage of being able to promote your own work.

Everyone involved in a cooperative benefits from fewer hours to work per partner, higher percentage of the retail price going to the artist, and personal access to customers that normally does not come from simply placing your work in a retail store or gallery. For more details on starting a cooperative crafts venture see Chapter 13.

The above ideas for selling your work are the easiest and least costly to you in expense. This is because they work according to how much you invest in effort, time, and personal contacts. If this way of selling seems too personal or threatening, try art and craft shows explained in Chapter 3. Here, the public comes to you and often buy on impulse without the trauma of knocking on doors.

Gathering ideas of what to make

By now, you may have already learned there's no shortage of craft projects to make. The challenge is to find which art and craft products sell and decide whether you want to make them. So how do you find out what the public is buying?

Look at what consumers are buying at art and craft fairs. This involves going to a show and walking around taking notes of which booths are the busiest. You can also try talking to some of the artisans and asking them, but don't imagine that they will welcome your entering the marketplace as a competitor.

I was fortunate to begin my crafts education with a weaver/artist who had been selling her work at shows for some years. She wove garments using colors and designs inspired from her years as an artist and had found, over time, which garments and color combinations sold well. When I was beginning, she let me weave her designs until my own creativity awoke.

Learn what's selling in retail stores and galleries. Almost all store owners, when they aren't busy, are anxious

Figure 1.0 Magazines and periodicals that feature arts and crafts products and supplies.

Aardvark Territorial Enterprise
American Artist
American Craft
American Woodworker
Art Material Trade News

Arts & Crafts Newsletter
BackHome
Barbara Brabec's Self-Employment Survival Letter
Better Homes & Gardens

Boy's Life
Bridal Crafts
CWB: Custom Woodworking
Candlelighter
Ceramic Arts & Crafts
Ceramic Hobbyist
Ceramics Monthly
Child Life
Children's Digest
Children's Playmate
Chip Chats
Classic Toy Trains
Constantine's Woodworking
Counted Thread
Country Accents
Country Almanac
Country America
Country Business
Country Decorating Ideas
Country Extra
Country Folk Art Magazine
Country Handcrafts
Country Home
Country Journal
Country Living
Country Magazine
Country Victorian Accents
Country Woman
Countryside
Craft Marketing News
Craft Trends/Sew Business
Crafts 'N Things
Crafts Magazine
The Crafts Report
Creative Crafts and Miniatures
The Creative Machine
Crochet World
Cross Stitch & Country Crafts
Cross Stitcher
Cross-Stitch Plus
Decorating Digest
Decorative Arts Digest
Doll Collector Price Guide

Early American Life
Family Circle
Family Handyman
Fine Woodworking
First For Women
Good Housekeeping Magazine
Harrowsmith
Harrowsmith Country Life
Highlights for Children
Hobby Merchandiser
Homemakers Magazine
Hopscotch Magazine
House Beautiful
Interior Design Magazine
International Doll World
Journal of Light Construction
Just CrossStitch Magazine
Knitting World
Ladies' Home Journal
Lady's Circle
Lapidary Journal
Leather Craftsman
Life Magazine
McCall's
Metropolitan Home
Miniature Showcase
NatureScope
Needle People News
New Home
New Woman
New Women's Times
News Basket
Now Magazine
Nutshell News
Old Time Crochet
Ontario Craft News
Profitable Crafts Merchandising
Parade Magazine
Piecework
Plastic Canvas World
Popular Woodworking
The Professional Quilter
Quick & Easy Crafts

Quick & Easy Quilting
Quilt World
Quilter's Newsletter
Redbook
Rug Hooking
Sampler & Antique Needlework
School Shop
Sew News
Sewing Update
Shuttle Spindle & Dyepot
Sourcefinder
Southern Accents
Southern Vermont
Star
Stitch 'N Sew Quilts
Stitches Count
Stylepages
Talent Company
Threads
Today's Lifestyles
Today's Woodworker
Tole World

Toy & Hobby World
Treadleart
Vantage Magazine
Wearable Wonders
Weaver's
Weekend Woodcrafts
Wildfowl Carving & Collecting
Woman's Day
Woman's World
Women Today
Women's Circle Crochet
Women's Household
Women's Household Crochet
Woodenboat Magazine
Woodsmith
Woodworker
Woodworker's Journal
Workbasket
Workbench
Yankee Magazine
Your Big Backyard
Zillions: Consumer Reports/Kids

(Check your library, bookstore or craft supplier for these publications. See the Appendix for addresses of the major magazines).

---

to talk about what moves well and what doesn't. They are constantly on the look out for new merchandise. Ask them what sells in their store. If you are prepared to show them your work at the time, you might even get your first order this way. See Chapter 4 for more about selling to stores.

Look for inspiration of product ideas (don't blindly copy them) in magazines and periodicals. If none come to mind, see the following list which doesn't include newspapers which sometimes feature arts and crafts in their Arts & Entertainment sections.

Almost all crafts have at least one magazine devoted to the field. Craftwork you see in magazines or at fairs is good inspiration. Be aware, however, copyright laws prohibit copying another's designs or patterns.

Another way to find out what the public is buying is to look at the current consumer trends as reported by companies that measure them. For instance, Americans annually spend around $35 billion on clothes, over $6 billion on art, and over $10 billion on jewelry. These kinds of statistics are sometimes found in *The Wall Street Journal, American Demographics* Magazine, or other business periodicals. The Gallup Organization, Box 310, Princeton, NJ 08542 does surveys on a wide variety of consumer areas. Another source is *The Public Pulse,* a monthly newsletter by The Roper Organization, 205 E. 42nd St., 17th Fl., New York, NY 10017. Both of these services charge for their information and reports; write them for more information.

Identifying customers

Craft fairs are the obvious place to locate customers to sell crafts to. Suppose, though, you want to sell more. You can easily spend all your time and money trying to sell your products to anyone and everyone. Not everyone, however is interested in arts and crafts. To avoid wasting resources, it helps to create a list of groups that your particular product fits within. Call these groups 'Broad market categories.' Of course, one item may fall into several groups. An example list of categories for buyers of arts and crafts might include: 1) Home & Garden, 2) Clothing, 3) Accessories, 4) Interior designers, 5) Corporate, 6) Graphic arts, 7) Toys, 8) Religious, 9) Jewelry, 10) Special Occasion, 11) Other

After you have come up with a list of the different groups, think about all the different items that could be sold to each market. Figure 1.1 is an example of lists of products that fit under the various broad market categories.

These lists show items that the public buys with space provided to write in your own ideas. A list like this gives you a clear picture of what's possible and practical in making and selling arts and crafts. Note that the order in which the items appear on this sample does not reflect their sales, ease of production, or profitability.

Figure 1.1 List of art and craft products by broad market categories.

Home & Garden	candles, placemats, napkins, curtains, towels, potholders, coasters, fire screens, baskets, pillows, quilts, room dividers, coverlets, throws, wall hangings, carvings, floor rugs, lamps, chairs, swings, stained glass, birdhouses, wind chimes, clocks, mirrors, cutting boards, pottery, plant holders, window boxes, potpouri
Clothing	dresses, shawls, blouses, aprons, suits, kimonos, children's clothing, men's and women's: shirts, vests, ruanas, sweaters, jackets, coats, painted sweatshirts, t-shirts
Accessories	handbags, purses, belts, sashes, babushkas, mittens, mufflers, house slippers, men's ties, men's and women's: scarves, hats, caps, bandannas, boots, sandals, moccasins

Interior design	paintings, wall hangings, rugs, upholstery fabric, throws, curtains, passementeries, pillows, room dividers, screens, window frames, furniture
Corporate	rugs, tapestries, wall hangings, sculpture, furniture, stained glass, paintings, batiks, folk art, carvings, flower arrangements
Graphic Arts	stationery, books, calendars, gift cards, note cards, posters, caricatures, buttons, bumper stickers, photo prints, signs
Toys	stuffed toys, dolls, puppets, animals, wooden trains, puzzles, building blocks, toy boxes, kaleidoscopes
Special occasion	bridal gowns and shawls, baby blankets, greeting cards, Christmas ornaments, stockings, Easter bunnies, heart pillows for Valentine's day, wreathes
Religious	altar objects, vestments, tapestries, chalice palls, baptismal towels, banners, stoles, stained glass, candelabras

| Jewelry | earrings, bracelets, necklaces, rings, anklets, headbands, jewelry cases, leatherwork, nose rings |

| Other | tote bags, duffel bags, backpacks, garment bags, saddle-blankets, musical instruments, dried flowers, book ends, confecitonaries, keyholders, seatcovers |

That's over 120 items. Of course, it's impractical to try to produce this many different craft items without employing others. For a one-person shop, it's more reasonable to concentrate on one or two markets and a spread of products aimed at particular buyers.

You will achieve more by channeling your energies and resources toward the group(s) of purchasers most likely to buy your craft products. If you try to make too many different items, or try to sell to those who don't want your products, you dissipate your momentum and waste time and money.

The practical approach is to find a few things that sell well and concentrate on building a 'bread and butter line.' Make products that sell steadily to earn the money to stay in business from month to month. Once you have established that wonderful menu of income-producing products, you can expand into other products and develop new designs. If you can adjust to working with employees, hire others to produce or do the finishing process.

Sales channels

Sales channels are the different ways to reach your buyers. You have already created a list of markets and products.

Now write down all the possible ways to reach each group. Suppose you want to know at a glance how many ways are there to sell handmade jewelry? Look at this example:

Figure 1.2 Channels to sell your products

<u>Category</u>	<u>Item</u>	<u>Selling Channel</u>
Jewelry	earrings	craft shows, renaissance shows, mall shows, stores, craft malls, sales reps, mail order, catalogs, gift trade shows, other trade shows, county and state fairs, studio sales, cooperative galleries, home parties, door-to-door (any other ideas?)

Make a market list for every product you have thought of making. Which products offer the most opportunities for sales? Keep these lists and add in new ideas as they come.

You may suspect that many products in Figure 1.1 might not have a large enough market to turn a profit. This is true. But how can you know ahead of time? Several influences affect a product's salability. Look at your product ideas in relation to the elements that follow.

Does the piece have a function that makes it useful to a person in daily life? Does it fill a basic human need or will the piece be sold as decorative art? Everyone has needs. They will buy something they can use before they buy a piece of art. Also, they will buy something they can wear before they buy a piece of furniture and they will usually buy something to eat before they buy anything else.

Basic human motivations

The well known humanistic psychologist, Dr. Abraham Maslow developed a theory of human motivation that says that everyone is motivated by a set of needs and that these needs can be classified into various levels of importance.

The first level is our physiological needs for food, drink, sleep, exercise, and so on. The second level is our safety or security needs; protection against threat, danger, or deprivation. Level three is our social needs; those are the needs for belonging, acceptance, love, and friendship. Level four, ego needs, refers to the needs for self confidence, achievement, status, recognition, and respect from others. Level five is self fulfillment, the need to realize one's potential, to create, and to experience personal growth and peak experiences.

Once a person satisfies a need, that need no longer motivates them. If a need is frustrated, however, it becomes important. Advertisers and marketing experts make use of these needs when designing promotional material. They attempt to seduce us into buying their products by stimulating one or more of the basic needs.

By looking at each product or promotional idea in view of this theory, you can see how a customer's buying priorities will be arranged. Does your product fill one or more of these needs?

It helps to translate the needs into more general terms like freedom from fear, health, emotional comfort, more money, being popular, convenience, entertainment, someone to love, time, sexual fulfillment, pride, physical comfort, attractiveness, prestige, and so on.

Evaluate your products against the list and see if they help meet any of the basic needs. A handmade quilt or bedspread might a) keep you warm, b) be attractive, c) have value as an heirloom, d) be worthy of pride, e) a subject of entertaining conversation, and f) be convenient to use.

Many new products fail when introduced into the marketplace because they lack familiarity. This is because if a person feels threatened or uncomfortable, it impinges on the important basic need for safety or security. Often, something new or unheard of, raises doubt or subtle anxiety. Take an item that feels familiar,is of time proven use, add a new twist or design element, and you may have a winner.

Wherever archeologists uncover ruins, they always find jewelry, pottery, inlays, bits of weavings, and other crafts. In the not too distant past, everything was handmade. Now, we consider handcrafted work a collectible novelty.

There is another need that is typically American and equally important to know about. You can see the evidence of it at any good crafts show. We are part of a consumer society. We feel a need to spend money. As my parents used to say whenever I ran out and spent my allowance, *"That money's burning a hole in your pocket."* The public is going to spend money anyway, so it might as well be with you.

Geographic location

Where will you sell your arts and crafts? Location affects the sales of many items. Goods like rugs, placemats or coasters are found in homes everywhere. Clothing items like sweaters, on the other hand, are going to sell better in states with colder weather. You probably won't sell as many scarves in Phoenix and San Diego as you will in Boston or Chicago. Sweatshirts, however, are worn almost everywhere.

Craft products for the home or office, jewelry, and toys will be affected less by geography than by clothing and wearable accessories. Sometimes, locations can seem uninviting for your product, but ironically yield good results. For example, woven horse saddle blankets might not seem to fit well in New York City, yet thoroughbred horse shows are well attended there.

If your product has nationwide appeal, you can plan sales efforts on a big scale. Just because an item sells only in a specific area of the country, it isn't necessarily a handicap.

You can target specific geographical niche markets when you can't afford to sell all across the country. In any case, focusing on your audience's particular needs is the key to using your resources more effectively.

Demographics

Demographics are elements like age, sex, family style, occupation, income, and religion. For instance if you make dolls, the largest group of buyers will be parents and relatives of children. If you make needlepoint or woven tapestries with religious images, your sales efforts will be directed to church groups. Obviously, an item that appeals to the most groups will have the biggest sales. If jewelry is your line, almost all of your sales will be to women. In fact, women are the largest group of consumers for any products. This is true for home items as well as clothing and other craft pieces. Design displays and write promotional material remembering you must often appeal to women's preferences.

Season

Some products can be marketed only at certain times of the year. Like geographic location, clothing sales are the most likely to be influenced by season. Home and office sales follow normal retail selling trends throughout the year. For most craft items, you can expect to do half or more of your annual business from fall through Christmas. These are the months for biggest retail sales of almost all products. Craft items that fall into the special occasion category can be marketed more effectively in the weeks before their occurrence. Greeting cards with cross-stitch or woven inserts lend themselves well to seasonal and holiday buying. The most popular card sending holidays are in order, Christmas, Valentine's Day, Easter, Mother's Day, and graduation. An inexpensive card with hearts in the design will sell well because customers don't hesitate to spend a couple of dollars to say *'I love you'* to Mom, a friend, or a sweetheart. They are a perfect gift item at an inexpensive price. Christmas is the season for all kinds of gift items, ornaments, and wreaths. Craft magazines are full of holiday ideas to inspire you for seasonal creating.

Wholesale or retail?

Will you sell your product wholesale to stores or will you sell retail at craft shows, home parties, and mail order? What if you want to do both? At first, you can only guess

Figure 1.3 Overlapping variables that influence sales

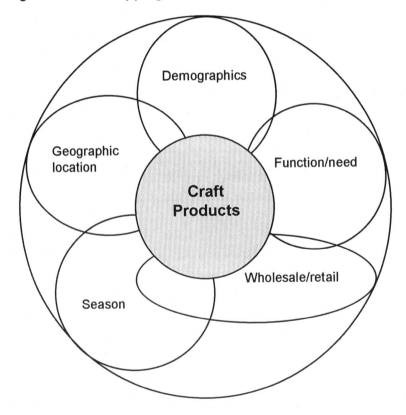

which of your products will do best in any particular market. Later, by keeping track of sales, you can see how some pieces will not work at crafts shows, yet sell excellently in stores and galleries. Since selling to stores usually requires more formal business practices than selling at craft shows, see Chapter 4 for what you can expect from running a wholesale business.

Overlapping effects

Often you will find the above mentioned variables overlapping each other's influence. For instance, if you create sweaters, the apparent place and season for best sales are states where the weather is cooler. But, Florida and Arizona attract vacationing 'snow birds' (tourists from the northern states who go south for the winter) who will buy sweaters in shops there to take back north. My best store account for selling wool and mohair wraps was in San Antonio, Texas, a burgeoning convention city with a constant influx of northern visitors in the winter months.

Understand the variables and plan ahead to take advantage of prime opportunities. Any artisan's business will benefit from considering the above mentioned elements. Decisions about what to make will change with experience, instincts, and the amount of resources you have to work with. Choices will change, too, as you learn what you can produce and what you want to produce.

The original title of this chapter was: *Wondering What Sells? How About Mohair Shorts?* This started as a joke between another weaver and myself about what she should make for her boyfriend's birthday. You may or may not think the idea of selling mohair shorts is amusing, but consider this: how often do customers buy unusual gifts as a joke? Sometimes the weirder the idea, the more appeal it has. If anyone tries this idea, let me know how it goes, I'm itching to find out.

Chapter 2
How to Price Your Work

Many artists and craftspersons are shy about charging enough for their work. If you intend to stay in business longer than three to four months, it's important to look closely at how much you're asking for your craft work and how you came to this decision.

Will you sell wholesale, retail, or both? Wholesale means selling products to someone who, in turn, marks up the prices and then sells the items to the public. Examples are stores, galleries, and catalog companies. Retail means you sell your work direct to the public such as at art and craft shows, home parties, by mail order, or from your studio or retail store.

There is no law that says you must restrict your business to one or the other. You may want to, though, once you learn the differences between the two ways of selling and which you enjoy most. Many craftspersons do business at both levels. It isn't difficult to do this as long as you keep the distinction between wholesale and retail pricing clear.

A common situation arises at many craft shows — a store buyer suddenly appears and asks if you sell your work to stores. She wants to know your wholesale prices, payment terms, and when you can deliver. Are you ready with the answers? If you are unprepared, this situation can put you off balance and you could easily lose another possible outlet for your work. This chapter helps you find exactly how much to charge in either wholesale or retail environments.

Average market price

The average market price for a given product is what most artisans sell similar work for. This is also called the ceiling price. If you plan to sell at craft shows, go around to several and check prices that similar craft items are selling for. Make a list totalling all the different prices you find, then divide this figure by the number of items in the list. When you have found the average price, you have the ceiling or the most you want to ask for your work.

If you exceed the ceiling price by too much, sales will suffer. If you charge much less, the same could happen because you have 'cheapened' the value of the piece in the eye of the consumer who has probably seen your competitors products at a higher price.

It is important to remember that purchasers of arts and crafts are collectors, as well as buyers. If they really want a bargain, they'll go to Wal-Mart.

Check retail prices for the same items in stores and galleries, too. You can assume that the price the store is asking is twice what they actually paid for the item. If you want to sell to stores, can you afford to sell your work at those prices? Figuring the floor price which is explained shortly will tell you if you can.

You could use the ceiling amount as a pricing strategy indefinitely. If you intend to do mostly craft shows, all you need to know is how much the average customer is willing to pay for a given product.

Note that prices will usually differ between a retail store and a craft show for the same item because of the store's higher operating expenses. For example, you may find the average price of a handmade coat priced at $400 in galleries and similar coats priced at $300 at craft shows.

When I first began selling my work, I was uncomfortable pricing my pieces as high as everyone else. Because I lacked confidence, I was settling for lower income. It was not long, though, before I became painfully aware of the need for getting full dollar value for my efforts. Looking at the expenses incurred from the shows, my labor, and my overhead, I found I was producing quality pieces for less than minimum wage. If your sales are high, but you still aren't making a profit, find exactly what it costs you to make a piece and to sell it. Knowing that, you can then make intelligent choices as whether to stop producing unprofitable items or find ways to make them at a lower cost.

Floor price

While the average market price for your products is the ceiling price or the most you will charge, the formulas below will give you the floor price or the lowest price you can safely charge for an item, insuring that you make a fair profit. To find the floor price, you must learn the production cost or what it costs to make an item, plus what it costs to sell it. Production cost is the sum of indirect costs, labor costs, and materials costs. Following is an explanation of these expenses. Figuring cost of sales is covered afterward.

Indirect costs

Indirect costs are those expenses necessary to keep the business running on a daily basis. These include tools, equipment, rent, utilities, travel expenses, insurance, and so on. When just starting business, estimate what these costs will be for a year's time. Some expenses like travel, advertising, or shipping costs will vary from month to month because of your show schedule. You might do more shows in the summer and fall than in winter. Within the first six months, though, you will get a better idea of how much money is needed to keep things going.

Figure 2.0 Sample list of indirect expenses.

Expenses	Per month	Per year
accounting	$ 25	$ 300
advertising	$ 10	$ 120
auto	$100	$1,200
cartons		
electricity	$ 25	$ 300
freight	$ 20	$ 240
heat	$ 25	$ 300
insurance	$ 30	$ 360
interest & bank fees	$ 20	$ 240
laundry	$ 15	$ 180
legal expense		
licenses		$ 40
misc. exp.	$ 30	$ 360
office	$ 10	$ 120
postage	$ 8	$ 96
rent	$250	$3,000
repairs	$ 10	$ 120
selling	$ 35	$ 420
telephone	$ 25	$ 300
trade dues		
travel	$100	$1,200
wages		
water	$ 12	$ 144
TOTAL	$750	$9,040

Total indirect expenses for this example equals $9,040.

Labor costs

After you figure the indirect costs, the next amount to determine is the cost of labor. This is the hourly wage you pay yourself and if you hire employees, what you pay them. When calculating the amount you pay others, add 30% of their hourly rate to cover social security, other payroll expenses, and accounting time.

As an example, say that you pay yourself $10 per hour, a fair amount to start with as a base. If you work alone and only 40 hours a week, 48 weeks a year, the total number of hours worked in one year is 1,920. Multiply this times $10 and you get a total annual cost of labor as $19,200.

Cost of materials

Cost of materials is the amount spent on materials, including accessories, to make an item. Don't include, however, tools or equipment which comes under indirect costs. Here is an example for figuring material costs of a rag rug that is 32" by 48". Weight of the rags used comes to 3 pounds. Cost of the pre-cut rags was $1 per pound, making a total of $3 in rags. You used 1/2 pound of yarn at $5 per pound plus .05 cents worth of sewing thread for finishing. Adding $3 + $2.50 + .05 gives a materials cost of $5.55 for one rug.

Now, double that amount. This is the necessary profit to collect on materials to insure you make the same markup a retail outlet charges a customer. Total materials cost is $11.10 for one rug.

Production cost

We now want to find the total amount it costs to produce one rag rug. Add the total indirect costs of $9,040 to the labor costs for one year, $19,200 and the total is

$28,240.00. This is what it costs to operate your business for one year. Divide $28,240 by the number of work hours, 1,920, to give an hourly cost of doing business of $14.71. If one rug takes two hours to make, multiply $14.71 times two to give $29.42. Add in $11.10, the cost of materials to equal a total production cost of $40.52 for one rug.

Cost of sales

Now you have the cost of making one rug, but before setting an accurate price, you need to know how much it costs to sell the piece. Cost of sales is easy to figure. For example, say that you sold the rugs through 18 art and craft shows last year. Also, say that you spent an average of 30 hours per show, including driving, setup, the hours of the show, tearing down and the drive home. Total hours spent to sell the rugs for the year were 540. If you sold a total of 360 rugs, divide 540 by the number of rugs, 360, to get an average time of 1.5 hours selling time per rug. At an hourly rate of $10 an hour, it cost $15 to sell one rug.

Setting the retail price

It cost $40.52 to make the piece and $15 to sell it, making the total expenses $55.52 per item. This amount is the floor price or the least to charge to insure a fair profit when selling at crafts shows or to other retail customers. If you set the retail price anywhere between $75 and $100, you have a spread of between $20 and $45 to bargain with or to keep as profit. At craft shows, you often encounter the time-honored tradition of bargaining. Should you drop your prices in order to make extra sales? Once you know the floor price, you can build in a bargaining cushion to your prices. At good shows, I have taken in as much as $400 or more by reducing my prices near closing time when customers come around to look for last minute deals. I knew my floor price and how low I could go in order to please the bargainer and still make a profit.

At craft shows, you can also test your prices from show to show and at different times of the year to see at what point the price affects sales. Typically, setting a slightly higher price, within reason, will work to your advantage. This is because customers tend to assign higher value to more expensive items.

Setting wholesale prices

Pricing strategy is not much different for sales to wholesale accounts than at craft shows. For example, say you sold 400 rugs through stores or catalogs last year and you spent 20 hours making sales calls to get the accounts. Divide 20 hours by 400 rugs to get an average of three minutes to sell each rug. Multiply this times an hourly wage of $10 and the average cost of sales is $.50 per item. Add this $.50 to the production cost of $40.52. This yields a wholesale floor price of $41.02. Stores normally arrive at their retail price by doubling their cost of what they buy. This is known as 'keystoning'. For example, a store pays you $41.02 for one rug and marks it up to $82.

Now, before you go trying to sell your rag rugs to stores, consider the total picture. Since rag rugs are available and inexpensive at many large department stores, you probably won't find many retail shops willing to pay $41.02 per rug.

Should you then forget about making rag rugs? Not necessarily. Consider making one-of-a-kind rugs and selling them to interior design stores. Look for other markets like galleries, where your better rugs will be considered art instead of home products. In the right setting, the customer sees the work's artistic value and does not make the department store comparison. In these cases, you can sell pieces to the gallery and still make a profit.

Item profitability

Creating an item profitability chart as the one in Figure 2.1, for each of your products shows at a glance which item brings the most profit in a given market. This gives an overall view of where you make the most money. Use this information to decide what to make and where to sell. See in this example that sales through catalogs are losing money. This suggests dropping the catalog market and doing more craft shows or approaching more interiors stores. A chart like this will help set criteria for making more profitable decisions based on your active selling experiences.

Figure 2.1 Item profitability chart

ITEM PROFIT TABLE FOR: Rag Rug				
MARKET	Sales Amount	Production Cost	Cost of Sales	Profit
CRAFT SHOWS	75	40.52	15.00	19.48
HOME SHOWS	75	40.52	7.00	27.48
INTERIORS STORES	45	40.52	0.50	3.98
REPS	45	40.52	21.50	-17.02
CATALOGS	49	40.52	18.50	-10.02
OTHER				

What happens when you find through your calculations that a product is losing money? Examine the costs of producing it. Can you save on labor or materials costs in any way you haven't considered. Sometimes production time can be cut by doing more products at one time. Possibly you can lower materials costs by buying in larger quantities to receive a discount from suppliers. If you find there is no way to reduce your costs on a losing item, it is better to drop the item completely and focus on more profitable pieces.

One-of-a-kind pieces

If a piece is one-of-a-kind or part of a limited edition series, setting the price must account for the intrinsic or artistic value in addition to the basic pricing information in the formulas above. How do you put a price on your art? If you are new at the business, try to find similar pieces by several other artisans and stay in that range. By the time you become famous, your work will have found its own price level. In a free market system, the dollar value of art seems to rise with the reputation of the artist.

You can get by for a long time with guesswork about how you're doing with pricing your work. However, if you wonder why you have plenty of sales, but aren't making a profit, you need to do the kind of analysis we have looked at here.

Chapter 3
Succeeding at Art & Craft Shows

Though today's craft fairs are looked on as a source of handcrafted novelties and collectibles, the outdoor market is probably the oldest historical business tradition known. Many made their crafts and foods and brought them to the marketplace to sell or trade. Even now in other countries around the world, the common market is a major part of daily life.

We in the U.S. have our own tradition known as 'the shopping mall.' The American public seems obsessed with shopping. People love to shop. Some of them even like to buy, but what they enjoy most is the lively activity of a marketplace. This excitement of shopping is even more present in the art and craft shows. When you wander around a craft fair today, you can sense an excitement from artisans selling their exotic hand made wares and seekers hunting treasures at a bargain.

A craft show is a good starting point for anyone selling their work. Beyond the dates of the show, there are no further commitments. When a show is over, it's over. You can do one or two and walk away with a minimum of expense of time and money or you can do shows every month and take up the craft fair life-style, making it the mainstay of your business.

In an art and craft fair, you have your own scaled down model of a retail store, even if it's only for two or three days. You can use a show to test new products, designs, price changes and booth displays. You are directly in touch with the marketplace, so if your work isn't selling, you will find out why immediately from customers' reactions and sales results.

In selling direct to the public, you keep the entire amount of the sales, minus expenses. Since almost all shows are held on weekends, your week is free to create more pieces. You have control of your time. It's a great feeling to go to a movie in the middle of the week when everyone else is laboring under canned air, moronic managers, and minimal wages.

How to find shows

There are several resources that list art and craft shows around the country and give information about show performance in previous years. If you buy these guides, and you should, get the most current editions available. Show performance changes over the years due to causes you have no other way of knowing about. Some shows simply fold up and disappear. Compare different reviews for the same show. If the reports are similar among various guides, then you can consider them good bets.

The Appendix lists almost all of the major guides. They may seem expensive, but you can make back or save hundreds of dollars more than the cost of these books by selecting or avoiding a show because of what you learn from them. Avoiding the bad shows is worth the price alone. In addition to show guides, announcements of events can be found in periodicals like *Sunshine Artists, The Crafts Report,* and *Southern Arts & Crafts. Sunshine Artists* gives reviews every month on shows in states where they have craftspersons reporting. *The Crafts Report* also gives sales and attendance figures of the bigger craft and wholesale shows after the event.

The Philadelphia Craft Show held in November is considered to be one of the better shows in the country. In 1993, average sales for exhibitors were $9,200 for wood, $14,700 for jewelry, $5,000 for furniture, and $10,585 for wearable fiber. For an application and more information, write The Philadelphia Craft Show, Box 7646, Philadelphia, PA 19101.

Another source of art and craft shows will be your state arts council. They should be listed in the government pages of your phone book. If not, write the National Assembly of State Arts Agencies, 1010 Vermont Ave. NW, Suite 920, Washington, DC 20005 for information on your state's organization.

Do your first show close to home, within one hundred miles. There are two good reasons; lower gas and mileage expenses, and less stress. A shorter drive and a longer night's sleep give you more energy for the show. Shows can be both exciting and demanding. Hundreds, possibly thousands, of potential customers come by your booth, many of whom will look at your work and talk to you.

If possible, visit a show beforehand to see if it attracts the right crowd for what you're selling. If you can't go in person, ask a friend that lives nearby to go. If that's not possible you'll have to rely on asking other craftspersons and information found in the craft show guides. Usually, if several exhibitors tell you a show is good, then it's probably safe to try the event once. Of course, some events are better than others. American Craft Enterprises puts on some of the largest shows several times a year with sales per booth averaging from $4,000 to $25,000. Their shows offer both retail-to-the-public sales days and wholesale-to-stores days. See the Appendix for their contact information. Many artisans try to get into these shows, so competition is intense. In these bigger shows, it is not unusual to suddenly find yourself taking more orders than you are used to filling.

Kinds of shows

When selecting shows, choose the kind of event that will attract buyers of the products you make. There are several different kinds. One is fine arts, only. Another kind of show is the juried art and craft fairs. A third kind is known as country craft shows. Crafts are also sold at a variety of other events such as state and county fairs, mall shows, renaissance fairs and large trade shows. Trade shows are discussed fully in Chapter 5.

● Fine art shows feature paintings, photos, posters, prints, sculpture, and other fine art. Often fine art shows are found in combination with the better craft fairs in order to draw larger crowds.

● Juried art and craft shows are often the most lucrative market for the craftsperson. Because the event is juried, the crafts displayed tend to be better quality and higher priced. A juried show is one where slides or actual pieces of your work are judged by a jury committee who selects the best from hundreds of applicants. All of the finer art and craft events are juried to screen out mass made products from kits and imported items.

● Country craft shows are distinctly different from the juried art and craft shows, though you may not be able to tell this from some of the show guide reviews. To present the image of a high quality show, country craft show promoters often say they jury entries, too. However, their main criteria for entry is that you aren't selling assembled kits or imported products. The crafts exhibited are usually for the home, almost all of them easily produced, and selling from $2 to $50. These shows often work well for small inexpensive gift items. I have tried them with high-end crafts and did not do well. When selling higher priced items, choose the more established, juried art and craft shows.

- <u>Renaissance fairs</u> are outdoor events that include craft booths as a part of a total entertainment package. All the vendors dress in medieval costume and booths have the same theme. A variety of food, drink, jugglers, jousters, knights, and fair maidens abound at these festivals. Almost all renaissance shows run every weekend from one to two months. You are responsible for building a substantial booth in the medieval theme. It must be sturdier than normal craft shows, because it will be up for several weeks. Count on spending $1,000 to $2,000 for construction costs. Since you rent the space for most of the weeks of the show, you become a lessee or tenant. Management also takes a percentage of your sales. Sales can be slower than other kinds of craft shows because the renaissance fair is often an entertainment event first, and a place to buy crafts second. Renaissance shows are listed in *Renaissance Shopper Magazine,* P.O. Box 422, Riverside, CA 92502.

- <u>Historical theme shows,</u> like renaissance shows are costumed events that provide entertainment and crafts demonstrations. They are often put on by historical organizations to coincide with special heritage days festivals. Listings for these shows can be found in *Early American Life,* P.O. Box 8200, Harrisburg, PA 17105.

- <u>Mall shows</u> are listed in craft show guides and periodicals. They are usually produced by the mall management, a show promoter, or a local organization. These shows are usually part of a tour sponsored by a producer putting on events in one or several nearby states. Many exhibitors follow the circuit for several weeks, especially in the fall and pre-Christmas months. At mall shows, you usually find more fine arts than crafts. Many shopping centers have restrictions on what can be sold, because they don't want you to compete with their store merchants who pay substantial rents. I have been denied entry in some shows because I sold clothing. In general, few of these shows do well for high end crafts. My experience related below, however, was an exception. If you make smaller items in the $10 to $50 price range, you might do okay. Even though rental fees are cheaper, sales are often lower than amounts you might receive from craft shows. Promoters usually ask a space fee, plus a percentage of the sales.

A well known juried crafts show usually attracts far better attendance than a mall show. When you can't find a good show, malls remain an option for otherwise empty weekends. Mall shows might help, too, in slow months like January and February. One year, I tried a mall show in January with a promoter who did a circuit of malls in the Southwest. Her shows had received good reviews in *Sunshine Artists,* a magazine listing shows and reviews by craftspersons doing events around the country. This particular show was held in a busy shopping mall in Albuquerque. I decided to try it for the experience of something different and also because there were no other craft shows happening at that time of year.

The show went for four days, beginning at 10:00 AM and going till 9:00 PM. I was given a large space, much bigger than spaces at any crafts show I had ever done, perhaps 25' by 25'. The promoter encouraged me to bring a loom and demonstrate my weaving during the show. Many of the customers walking by who saw me working, stopped to look or ask questions causing a crowd to gather. Though I spent more time talking than I did weaving, I made several sales and received several special orders as a result of demonstrating. Total retail sales from the show were about $1,300. I picked up one wholesale account with an initial order of $500. Also, I was able to produce about $500 worth of inventory during the four days. My cost of doing the show came to about $150 and the location was close enough that I could drive home every night.

I decided to do the following week in another mall with the same promoter, in another nearby city. Sales were about $500 lower and the one lead I got to a wholesale account didn't work out. It turned into a long exhausting two weeks, but considering how dead January and February usually are, it was a good experiment.

Other kinds of events provide excellent alternative markets for arts and crafts that can be quite successful. These shows cater to a niche market rather than to several different kinds of products. You can find out about shows for any kind of business or interest group by looking in magazines devoted to that subject. See the list of periodicals in the Appendix. Also, your library will have a copy of the *Standard Periodical Directory* by Oxbridge, which lists magazines and journals by subject index. For other sources of special interest group shows, see the Appendix for Wholesale Trade Show Organizers. Some possibilities for special interest markets for your craft products include, but aren't limited to:

- <u>Local fashion shows.</u> Women's groups and charity organizations often produce fashion shows for original work. Call your chamber of commerce and check the library for listings of associations in your area. Visit the large hotels and convention centers and speak with their public relations person. They have schedules of upcoming shows and producers to get in touch with.

- <u>Home shows and boat shows</u>. Many major cities have a home show and a boat show at least once a year. Look for announcements in your newspaper.

- <u>Gift shows.</u> Gift shows exist for both consumers and store buyers, usually held in large convention centers. The Oasis Gift Show, a semiannual event in Phoenix, Arizona has over 900 exhibitors, many of them jewelers, but also a special section for crafts. Their address is Oasis, 1130 E. Missouri, Ste. 750, Phoenix, AZ 85014, (800) 344-1237. See the Appendix for more listings.

- <u>Flea markets.</u> In some cities, flea markets have grown to include smaller, inexpensive craftwork. Booth rental is not as high as craft shows and they draw big crowds. Check them out, though, before you sign up, because almost all flea markets are full of garage sale items. Around Christmas time, however, smaller priced craft pieces like ornaments and toys may do well.

What to look for before applying

Before you apply to a show, visit it yourself, read what the show guides say about it, and talk to other craftspersons who have done the event. Here's a list of things you need to find out.

✓   How many booth spaces are being rented for the whole show? A show with 500 booths will draw bigger crowds than a show with only 50.

✓   Is the show outdoors or inside? Has weather affected previous attendance?

✓   Is the show well known? Does the promoter advertise in the newspapers, on radio, billboards or TV? Better shows are successfully promoted as annual events. The public knows about them and returns faithfully every year to see what's new.

✓   What are the security arrangements? Many outdoor events have no effective way of guarding your merchandise. Unless you secure your booth from possible entry, you should count on packing up and taking your goods at the end of each day of the show. Indoor shows are safer in this regard. The building is locked at a given time and often, there will be an overnight guard.

✓   What kinds of crafts are exhibited? Is this the kind of show that attracts buyers for your craft?

I once did a show in Dallas produced by a promoter of several shows all around Texas. I picked this one because it got good reviews in the *Sunshine Artists Audit Book*. I had relatives I could stay with and it was on the way to Houston, where I had two larger shows lined up. At the time, I knew nothing about country craft shows, which this one was. I took in about $450 in sales for $270 in expenses. I was the only fine crafts showing, so there was little product recognition by the public attending the show. The crowd simply was looking for inexpensive whatnots. If I had researched it ahead of time, I would have come with lower priced items.

How to apply

Applications for shows will be mailed upon request from the show producers. Once you are on their mailing list, you will probably continue to receive applications for a few years. Many applications are due three to six months before the actual show date. Some larger events like the ACE (American Craft Enterprise) shows, may require jurying a year or more in advance.

Better shows are juried. This means that the artist must submit slides or photos of their recent work and possibly a photo of their booth display to the show producer, along with a jury fee.

Many craftspersons agree that jury fees are unfair. A well known craft show may receive more than 800 applications for as few as 200 booth spaces. If each applicant sends in a $15 jury fee, the show promoters receive $12,000 dollars before they even collect the booth rental fees. If you want to get into the better shows, you have to play by their rules.

If you read the rules included with the application blanks for many shows, you will often see a requirement that artists sharing booths pay an additional fee. I think this is unfair. If I invite a friend to help and bring some of her work, I simply apply for the show in my name and put my friend's work out without paying an additional fee.

However, this doesn't work at larger shows, especially trade shows. Confusion that results when a store buyer wants one artist's work over the other's could result in harsh feelings and possible financial altercations. Some show's sales are too good to risk violations that might bar you from future admission. Nevertheless, no show management will mind if you have helpers.

When two or more persons split the rent for a space at a craft fair, it is easier on each one's pocketbook. Not only are these cooperative ventures economically sound, they generate more enthusiasm and pleasure for everyone. Of course, you must get along with your partners.

How to better your chances of getting in

There is no guarantee that you will be accepted into a show with your first application. Shows you do once, though, will often give you preference for reentry. To better your chances of getting accepted in any show, follow these guidelines:

- Slides are often *the* chief component in your acceptance by a jury. With hundreds of applicants, it is the quality of your slides that gains you entry into a show. Find a photographer with experience in the arts and crafts field; *The Crafts Report* often has ads. Count on making several sets of slides of six to twelve different pieces, plus your booth display. Often, you will send off one set to apply for a show and need another set for other applications also due. Some shows do not return the slides until the day of the event.

- If you're required to submit actual samples of your work, be sure to send your most detailed pieces. Technical execution may outshine design elements. If a display is needed, assemble it at home first to make sure it is sturdy and does not distract a viewer from the work itself.

- Follow instructions in the application form, word for word. Fill the information in completely, either by printing clearly or typing. Slides should be labeled in accord with their guidelines. Protect slides in envelope protectors made for sending slides. Enclose your application, photos or slides, jury fee, if any, and a SASE. If you don't follow their directions, they won't consider your application.

- Apply early. Sometimes it's first come, first serve.

- Many juries look for consistency of style among pieces. This shows your concentration on developing artistic excellence within a medium or theme. They are sometimes turned off by pretty models or beautiful backgrounds when they feel their use is meant as a distraction.

- If you apply to the American Craft Enterprise shows, they will send you information on how to make better slides of your work. Since their shows are some of the best in the country, it is worth applying. Write to American Craft Enterprises, 21 S. Eltings Corner Rd., Highland, NY 12528 (800) 724-0859.

Last minute cancellations

Here's a tip for the brave and adventurous. Almost every show I have attended has had last minute cancellations or no-shows by exhibitors who paid for their booth, but for some reason cannot get there. Can you guess how easy it is to get a space early in the opening hours of the show? Few promoters will refuse to take your money to fill the space. Nevertheless, they will probably want cash up front, so be ready.

To get into shows this way you should come prepared to set up your booth at the last minute before the show opens to the public. I have heard of at least one craftsperson who never sends in applications for shows, but always uses the above method. I was able to get into two major selling shows because of last minute cancellations that I'd been unable to get into through the normal application procedure.

If you try this, though, take a quick look at the space before you hand over your money. If the spot is on the end of a long string of booths, sales can be too poor to pay your expenses.

Planning your show schedule

Shows in the three or four months before Christmas will *usually* produce higher sales than at other times. Some organizations hold craft events in the spring and again in the fall. The fall shows are often better. No matter when you start your business, budget enough money for shows in the pre-Christmas months as your highest priority. Plan your production so that you will have plenty of inventory on hand.

If you like doing shows and decide to travel more than a day's drive to get there, it makes sense to line up events en route, signing up for two or three shows, back-to-back in nearby areas. Some craftspersons produce their whole inventory in several months and then follow a circuit of shows, selling every weekend for the few months before Christmas.

A cautionary note; doing several events in a row can be exhausting. Even one show can knock you out for a day or two. Until you know what you can comfortably endure, be conservative with how many you sign up to do.

If you plan to sell your work to stores too, use the time between weekends of shows to visit shops where you are traveling. Store owners in other parts of the country can give you feedback on how your products will sell in different geographical areas.

It happens frequently that two shows you want to be in are scheduled for the same weekend. Unless you have a guaranteed spot in one of them, apply for both and wait to see which one accepts you. Your cost will be the two jury fees, but at least you're covered if one rejects your application. If you have a partner, you can split up and do two shows the same weekend.

Consider doing shows in cities where you have friends or relatives. If you have a place to stay free, why pay $30 a night for a motel? Of course, they might have kids, dogs, and lots of energy to talk.

You can often find decent motel rooms for around $25 a night. It requires some checking when you pull into town, so count on extra time for research. It's easier to find vacancies in the afternoon than it is to find them after dark. You can find lower cost motels on the outskirts of towns on truck routes or old state highways. Once you find a good motel, keep their business card for future trips. It's a great relief to know you have a comfortable room ahead of you after hours of driving or doing a show.

To make your show planning easier and more efficient, get a big map of the United States and a large wall calendar with all the months of the year on one page. Use the calendar to show dates and deadlines for applications. By referring to the road map, you can plot travel time and rest stops in advance. Also collect maps of cities and states you travel through. Your first time in a new town is the hardest. Next year, you'll know where to stay and how to get around the area.

High booth fees do not always guarantee the show will be a good selling one, though many of the better shows are more costly. Several promoters, like Harvest Festival and Steve Powers Shows, put on circuits of scheduled events for several months running. Booth rentals are higher than the average craft show, but they do extensive advertising, provide entertainment, and pull in good crowds. They prefer craftspersons to sign up for several shows on the tour, but some allow you to do one to test your sales.

One of these shows in Houston yielded the biggest weekend sales I ever had, but the next year and the following year, sales kept dropping and fewer craftspersons exhibited. Even the promoters felt the show wasn't happening anymore, so they dropped the show.

Stay on top of information on these changes by making friends with other craftspersons. The crafts grapevine is alive with good news and bad news about what's happening with different events and geographic locations.

AVOID FIRST-TIME SHOWS! I had heard this advice repeatedly and always followed the obvious logic. Many craft shows are annual events that the public has attended for several years. How can a new show expect to draw good crowds? One time a promoter called from a state where I had done a show two years before. He had 'great news' about their first venture into Albuquerque, fifty miles from me. Because I had exhibited with them before, I had first choice on a location.

He offered me an extra booth space if I demonstrated my craft. He also told me they were doing extensive radio, TV, billboards, and newspaper ads. So, I signed up for a double corner booth in the middle of the exhibit hall. It cost $200 to do the show and I sold nothing the entire three days. This was the last time I will ever do a first-timer.

The worst part about this show was being subjected to a constant barrage of persons coming by the booth trying to sell me something, including two charities, one flower girl, three candy hawkers disguised as boy scouts, three new craft co-op store owners and four promoters trying to fill booth space in *their* new shows.

My favorite line was *"We're almost filled now, but I think I can find you a space . . ."*

Because there are so many good events around, it seems as if everyone wants to get into the act. There has been a great proliferation of self styled promoters aiming to get rich off show rental fees from craftspersons. Some of these person's prime interest is to make a buck off you. Don't be misled by their hard sell tactics about getting in on the ground floor NOW! . . . while there's still space left.

No matter how carefully you have chosen and prepared for a show, you sometimes run into some real dogs. I still hear some of mine barking from way back. All you can do is think of it as a continuing education.

Booth location

In good shows it doesn't matter where you set up, you're going to sell. Typically, though, booth spaces on a corner, near the center, entrance or exit of a show are better selling spots than spaces on the aisles. Avoid getting near the food vendors or entertainment. Food is the number one seller at shows and not only are you competing for attention, you must deal with junk food being carried in and around your pieces. If there is entertainment, noise from loud music will not only distract customers, but also prevent you from being able to talk to others pleasantly.

Request booth locations with your application if you know where you want to be. I've had requests acknowledged often, despite the application stating otherwise. If you have done a show in the past, managers may give you the same location or at least, give your booth preference a higher priority. Last minute cancellations leave empty spaces. If your allotted space is unacceptable, ask the show manager if you can trade in the first hours of setting up. You won't be the only one looking to switch, so get there quick with your request. All they can do is say no.

Craft show booths aren't large. Many shows give you a single 10' wide by 10' long. Unless past experience has shown that you need a double space, it is unusual to get enough sales to justify renting two booths. Double the space means double the rent. Be sure when you are applying for the show, what the exact booth size will be. Make your display flexible enough to fit in a smaller 8' x 8' space, if that's all you will get.

Displaying your products

Design your booth to show your work in a neat, orderly arrangement. It should be easy and inviting for the customer to walk in and browse. Allow the product to help sell itself.

The fuller the display, the more you will sell, no matter what the product. Customers buy more from a full rack or table. If they see gaps, dishevelled garments or a scattered pile of items, they feel the work is picked over too much. Keep racks and tables neat the whole time of the show. It may mean going over to straighten merchandise many times during the day, but the customer should feel they are the first ones to see your work. Also, items displayed closest to the customer will be the easiest to sell.

Figure 3.0 Sample booth display layouts

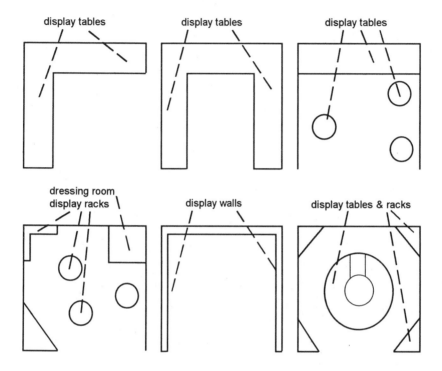

Place your most attractive pieces in the front of the fixtures or racks.

Use tables and hanging dowels for displaying blankets or throws, rugs, and other large flat items. They can be arranged in neat, clean stacks on the tables or in a waterfall descent from a standing display rack. Rugs look great this way. Shelves and tree displays show off dolls, ornaments, and whatnots. Customers can see some portion of every piece.

Look at crafts displayed in stores for ideas on how to show your work. This is a good way to learn how to display any item. Follow the examples of retailers who are already successful in selling hundreds of products to the public.

Also, visit craft shows and see how other craftspersons display their work. You'll change your display as you do more shows. Experiences will teach what works well and what doesn't. By my second year, I had changed my display at least seven times.

It is important that the booth make the customer feel free to enter. Build your display at home first, then play with variations of how the arrangement looks with your pieces displayed. You will have better success by carrying related products in your booth. For example, display all clothing related items, or have a booth that sells handbags, or all jewelry work. One of the attractions to the crafts show is access to small specialty shops. Too many different kinds of products together is distracting.

Arrange merchandise in product groups. Customers are used to shopping in stores where they can always see and find the colors they want. Offer a wide array of colors. A large selection will make some colors sell better than others.

Customers like variety. Experiment for a few shows with your arrangement and see how the public acts toward it. If you notice frequent hesitation or turning away from your display, try altering the arrangement to make it more inviting.

Every item should have a label and a separate hang tag with the price, your name, and address. Don't put the price on the label itself, because many of your sales will be given as gifts. A price tag on every piece is important. Some customers have the feeling of being cheated if they have to ask for the price of something. They wonder, too, if the person that comes along after them will hear the same amount.

If you have to divert your attention to answer one customer's question about price, another browser has an opportunity to walk away. Avoid this kind of loss by pricing and labeling everything in advance. Be ready to conclude a sales transaction quickly.

If you sell clothing or jewelry, have a mirror and a dressing room. Customers can then see how the piece looks on them. This is important. Get the person to try a piece on and the sale is halfway made. Fixtures, racks, grids, and tables can be used to hang or place your products on.

Metal or chrome fixtures may sell merchandise better than wood displays. Wood racks are more attractive and natural, but they also look more expensive. There is a subtle message conveyed to the customer that your fixtures are expensive, so your product must be, too. What is more important, the public is conditioned to shopping in stores with metallic fixtures. In every store carrying apparel, clothing is displayed on waterfall or descending spiral fixtures; all chrome, all shiny. By imitating the big retail experts, you can sell more to customers that are trained to buy from these kinds of displays. Take advantage of a consumer habit already in motion.

Used fixtures are found cheaply from stores going out of business. Watch your local newspaper classifieds. Some have a 'Fixtures' subheading. Many cities have used fixture stores where you can buy or rent at prices cheaper than you can buy new pieces. There are also fixture catalogs that you can order items by mail. Look for their ads in the craft magazines listed in the Appendix. Also, check the library for books listing catalogs.

Be sure your display can withstand the pressures of wind and constant customer handling. Also, they should be light enough that you can load and unload them from your car by yourself.

Booth cover

For protection against the sun and unexpected changes in the weather, acquire a canopy or covering that will adequately protect you and your pieces. You only need to get rained on once to realize how important this is. Use a frame and cover that is sturdy enough to withstand high winds, rain, and large crowds. White tarps or canvas work

Figure 3.1 Sample booth covers

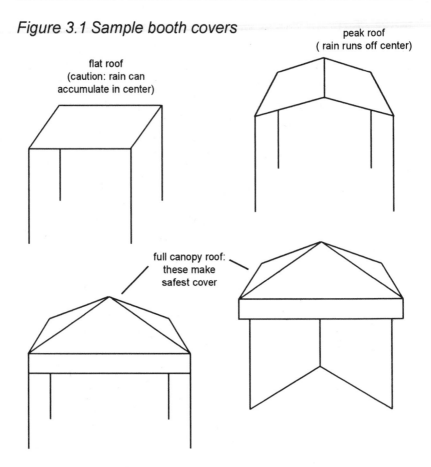

best, as colored tarps will cause the light to be tinted and affect the appearance of your merchandise.

You want adventure, danger, and suspense from a good movie, not from your booth covering. You could easily face a lawsuit, if your homemade frame blows down onto a customer's child or the potter next to you. At best, you'll find yourself the owner of a large collection of pottery shards. Physical safety of your customers, fellow craftspersons, and your own merchandise should be a priority in constructing your booth.

If you have a friend with tools and some construction skills, you can design a structure to suit your own needs.

But unless you are confident about your skills, save yourself the trouble by investing in a well known brand cover like the KD canopy. There are booth suppliers that sell displays ready to set up and designed for the craftsperson doing outdoor shows. A list of these companies is in the Appendix. Many of them run ads in periodicals like *The Crafts Report.*

Sometimes other craftspersons sell their fixtures or displays, either because they are buying better setups, or because they're not doing outdoor shows anymore. Other sources for booth setups are flea markets and the yellow pages under 'Tents and Awnings'.

Accepting credit cards

Credit card purchases can increase your sales by 30% to 40%. This is especially true for high ticket items at craft shows where the purchaser may not have enough cash or where tourists do not carry cash. As a credit card merchant, you pay a discount fee to the bank processing the transaction (usually 3% to 8%) on each sale. Recently my bank added a monthly minimum service charge of $15, applied against discounts of sales. This means, even if I have no credit card sales in a given month, I still pay a $15 fee.

Merchants either run each card through an electronic communications device or are required to call an 800 number for authorization when the sales amount is over a 'floor limit', usually $50, sometimes $75. This means sales under that amount do not require telephone approval. Also, you receive weekly a small booklet of lost, stolen or invalid card numbers. You can quickly check card numbers against this list before you conclude the transaction.

Advances have brought the cellular phone device that can be used by craftspersons at fairs. These portable credit card processors can be purchased or leased by companies that act as go-betweens for artists and the credit card companies.

The purchase price can be from $1,000 to $2,500 for such a unit, so you must do a lot of business to justify the expense. Two dealers that offer equipment are American Cardservice, 3303 Harbor Blvd., Costa Mesa, CA 92626 and Arts & Crafts Bankcard Services, 2804 Bishopgate Dr., Raleigh, NC 27613.

There are rules you must observe to maintain your merchant status. You are not allowed to deposit other merchant's sales. You cannot split large tickets into two smaller ones to avoid the floor limit check. Banks will give you a full list of the regulations. If you violate the bank's policies, they will close your account and it will be extremely difficult to renew your standing. To get merchant status, apply to a bank for a merchant account, almost all can accept credit card deposits. When you approach banks, be aware of the following:

- Banks get a discount fee of 3% to 8% of the total for each sale. Discount rates that the bank charges vary from bank to bank. Find out the various rates by calling the banks and asking what their credit card discount rates are for merchant accounts. Higher priced sales such as $150 might allow you a lower discount, but every bank has different rates and policies.

- There is a setup fee to get started; usually around $30 for the credit card machine and another $30 for supplies of sales and deposit tickets. In addition, some banks charge a service charge on a monthly basis, if your sales do not reach a certain amount. A typical charge is $15 per month.

- Banks don't like to give credit card accounts to mail order businesses or other kinds of business with high incidences or likelihood of fraud. If you tell them you do mail orders, you risk getting your application rejected.

- Merchants must have a physical business location, usually in the same county as the bank. They look for a street address, not a P.O. box. Set up your studio as a shop and make sales from there. This way if the bank wants to see a physical location, you can provide them with one.

- Banks prefer to work with their own customers. You should have been operating with a business checking account for at least one year. You need a business license, sales tax permit, a federal tax ID number and any other documents that prove you are a legitimate business.

An organization that can locate banks granting credit card merchant status is American Craft Association, 21 S. Eltings Corner Rd., Highland, NY 12528, (800) 724-0859.

My first year in business, I didn't accept credit cards. I thought it would be too difficult to get an account. Many craftspersons around me at the shows were taking cards, so I realized I was probably losing sales. Lots of cards were passing through those little credit card machines. When I started accepting credit cards, my sales picked up by 30%.

Accepting checks

As easy as credit cards might be for the customer, they cost you a percentage of the sale when they are used. You might do better to ask for a check. Tell customers you prefer to take their check instead of their credit card, but if they say no, don't push it. Accepting checks for payment has these advantages:

- You can easily record their address for your mailing list from the check.

- You don't have to pay a credit card discount (3% to 8%) of the sale to the bank.

● When doing an out-of-state show, you can check the banks they are drawn on to make sure they are good.

● You can cash checks locally for travel expenses.

Almost all bad checks are written on new accounts. The biggest percentage will have check numbers from 0 to 300. If you have doubts about a person, ask for a driver's license and a current phone number. Write the numbers on the top of the check or on the sales invoice.

State sales tax

Almost every state requires you to collect and pay a tax on each sale that you make. Some show producers include the state requirements in the application procedure. If not, contact the state you will be showing in several months in advance about getting a temporary permit. Sometimes states have local tax employees going from booth to booth, collecting estimates of your projected sales tax payments for the rest of the show. In some states, they expect you to abide by an honor system and mail in the computed tax amount after the show.

How to keep track of shows

Use a form like that in Figure 3.2 on page 65 to record information about each show you do. After you have done three or four shows, it's easy to forget details about a show you should remember for next year. Information on each sale is useful for tracking performance of different items, colors, and materials.

More tips for having a better show

✓ Create a mailing list of your customers' names and

addresses whenever someone makes a purchase or inquiry, enter their name on the list. When returning to the same city later, mail them a postcard with details of the show's date and if you know it, your booth location. You will find regular customers collecting your new pieces every year.

✓   Be prepared to wrap up the sale as soon as possible. At craft shows, the more time you spend with one customer, the easier it is for another one to walk away. Have bags handy to put the purchased item in.

✓   You will need a small space on a table to carry out the transactions. This will be where the customer can comfortably write a check or sign a credit card sales slip. Keep extra pens around. They inevitably disappear.

✓   Keep a receipt book for customers requesting one. By writing a receipt for every sale, you have a physical record and a copy to give to the customer. Also, legally you must give a receipt for each sale.

✓   Have a supply of brochures or flyers about you and your craft to give with each sale or inquiry.

✓   Bring extra ones, fives, and tens for making change. Keep your money in a belt concealed under your clothing. Never show large amounts of cash at the shows or motels you stay at when traveling. In larger cities, be extra careful when leaving the show to hide your money. Have a list of your credit card numbers at home or kept safe when traveling in the event you lose them.

✓   Consider buying a carpet remnant or rug for your booth. It looks good and gives you and your customers some relief from concrete floors at indoor shows.

√   Wear comfortable clothing; something you have made is the best promotion you can give your work. Also get a pair of comfortable sneakers.

√   Bring a lunch. The fewer times you leave your booth, the better chance of making sales. If you have someone to help you, it's easier to take breaks.

√   It helps if a friend or spouse can assist you. Setting up the booth and handling sales go more easily with two persons, but be careful not to impede the flow of traffic into your selling space. At some point, you will want to take a break, or walk around and see the other booths; this is impractical unless you have a partner.

√   Get a toolbox to keep emergency tools and supplies like scissors, electrical and duct tape, hammer, nails, pliers, screwdrivers, string or flexible wire, and spare parts for fixtures or booths. Keep a small box with needle, thread, crochet hook, and scissors for unexpected snags or just discovered mistakes. Include it in your toolbox.

√   For indoor shows, bring long extension cords, power strips, and clamp-on lights with bulbs. The better your lighting, the more you will sell. Most exhibit centers do not provide adequate light for good displays.

√   Flameproof your exhibit materials such as table covers and fabric backdrops. Almost all cities have strict regulations enforced by fire marshals inspecting each booth.

√   Make a checklist of the above items and go over it before you leave for the show.

Figure 3.2 Craft show report sample

CRAFT SHOW REPORT

DATE: 10/4/93	CITY: Boulder City		BOOTH: central	TYPE: craft show
TRAVEL TIME: 10 hours	IN/OUT? outside	#YRS 2	WEATHER: hot	CROWD: big
BOOTH FEE: $195	AUTO: $40	MOTEL: $50	ELECTRIC:	INSUR:
FIXTURES:	FOOD: $30	PARK:	OTHER:	TOTAL EXP: $315

QTY	ITEM	CONTENT	COLORS	SIZE	PRICE	SALE
1	jacket	cotton	dark mix	m	350	350
3	scarf	mohair	dark mix		65	195
2	rug	cotton	pastels	sm	75	150
2	cocoon	cot/rayon	blk/gold	lg	165	330
1	ruana	wool	maroon		135	135
3	blouse	cotton	pastels	m	95	285
1	scarf	wool	green/gold		40	40

COMMENTS: bring more light weight pieces, very warm weather, good show, nice crowd	SUBTOTAL	1,485
	LESS DISCOUNTS	
	TOTAL SALES	1485
	EXPENSES	315
	% EXPENSES TO SALES	22%

Awards

Many better craft shows offer prizes or cash awards for best display or best designer. One friend I worked with to help start her business won first prize in fiber arts at the *Dallas 500* show in Texas at her second show. Getting recognition is more than strokes for the ego, it adds value to your work in the eyes of customers. It also affords you speaking and teaching opportunities as a recognized professional artisan, another avenue for building demand of your work. Besides the publicity value, award winners often receive prize money. Many state fairs and some county fairs have juried events with large cash awards. Prestige you get from such awards will almost guarantee you feature articles in your local periodicals and newspapers. There is more on how to make use of this kind of free publicity in Chapter 6.

The more shows you do, the more often you will be approached by store owners looking for new merchandise. The next chapter helps you answer questions about selling to stores and galleries.

Chapter 4
Selling to Stores & Galleries

A direct approach is the easy way to get your work into stores or galleries. In many cities, I have had good results simply walking into a store and introducing myself to the owner or manager. I explain that I'm a fiber artist and ask if they are interested in looking at a few pieces of my work. Almost all of the time, they will look right then. It's easy for them to say *"No"* on the phone, but once you're standing in front of them, they ask, *"Do you have any pieces with you?"* I never walk in with the pieces however, it's too presumptuous and unprofessional and it only takes a minute to go back to the car.

Unless you have a specific appointment, avoid approaching stores on a Monday, Friday, or weekend. The best times are mornings in the middle of the week. Store owners are too busy or too tired in the afternoon, and they are often gone on weekends. The bigger the shop, the more likely they will want to make an appointment for another day. Stay flexible enough to work with their time frame. Never attempt to push your schedule on them.

If you're going to travel to sell to stores, send an introductory letter, brochure, photos, and a sample of your work ahead of time. Call about a week to ten days after you send the packet to confirm that it was received and set up an appointment.

If they will see you at a specific time, then you know you will meet with the person who makes the buying decisions. It's important that your personal appearance, promotional material, and the way in which your work is shown be clean and professional.

Here are some more tips to remember when approaching stores:

- If you make clothing, jewelry, or accessories, wear something you've made. The feedback you receive from store buyers is an excellent way to find out about pieces you should be making.

- Don't be late or early. If you don't show up on time, what will they imagine about delivery of your products? If you get there before they're ready for you, you will likely cause irritation.

- Before leaving home, check over your sample pieces for dust, cracks, open seams, scratches, wrinkles, and the presence of labels. Carry a small tool kit for repairing minor damages.

- Have your price lists, brochures, and business cards ready to give out. You also will need photos of your work and samples. Brochures are expensive, but they say 'professional'. See Chapter 11 for more on promotional material.

- Find an attractive display bag or suitcase for carrying your work into stores. Cardboard boxes and garbage bags present a poor image. I made a travel bag for protecting my woven clothing out of tapestry fabric.

Personalizing the relationship with the owner is an important part of building a wholesale business. It creates a comfortable feeling on both sides. It also helps when it comes to getting paid. If you have a positive rapport with an owner, they'll be more prompt with payment of invoices.

Finding stores

You may not have to look far to find wholesale accounts. It's inevitable that you will be approached by store owners at craft shows looking for new merchandise. After an owner or buyer approaches you, follow up by giving them a phone call to say thanks for stopping at your booth.

Make an appointment to meet with the owner and give a presentation. A good store account can provide steady sales for a long time. After establishing wholesale accounts, keep in touch with them. Sales will increase when you make more personal visits or telephone calls with the owners.

When I was first approached by a shop owner, I was selling ruanas, shawls, and sweaters at a craft show. She told me she owned several stores in the Midwest for larger size women's clothing.

My handwoven ruanas appealed to her and she asked me to call her the following week with wholesale prices and delivery times. I thought that at that time, I was having better sales at craft shows than I could get from working with stores. I put her card away, without giving it much consideration. I regretted this attitude later, when show sales slowed. By then, I couldn't find her card or remember her company's name.

After this loss, though, I was careful to follow up every lead. This resulted in several steady wholesale accounts that allowed me more time to produce at home and netted almost as much per piece as I was clearing from selling at craft shows.

Another time, my wife Dianne and I drove to Boulder, Colorado on the advice of another craftsperson we had met in Santa Fe. He was one of the jurors for an artist's cooperative gallery in Boulder. The size of the gallery, its annual sales, and location looked appealing.

The amount of weaving on display, however, discouraged us; six or seven local weavers were represented with a substantial inventory of scarves, clothing, rag rugs, and wall hangings. Walking down the street, we found two more such ventures; co-op galleries for local artists were definitely catching on. Again, we found more local weavers. Thinking there was just too much competition, we gave up our search and went to lunch.

Coming out of the cafe, Dianne noticed a shop that sold Santa Fe style crafts and gifts. We went in and saw a variety of moderately expensive southwestern arts and crafts similar to those selling in New Mexico, but no weaving. We were about to leave, when I suddenly thought to try to sell the owner on the idea of carrying our work which fit in well with her existing crafts.

She was interested, but only if we would leave pieces on consignment. Though I preferred to sell outright, I was anxious to test this market so close to outlets where competition was deeply entrenched.

In the first month, nothing sold. After one call back to the store, I neglected to check with them again, being busy with shows and other projects. At the end of two months, I had almost forgotten the account. This was not a good move.

One Saturday, the owner called to tell me she was sending a check for three pieces. She had sold the most expensive jackets we made and she wanted more things ASAP! The moral is: it pays to keep in touch with your store accounts on a regular basis, even when you think nothing is happening. And, it also pays to be assertive if you see an opportunity to open new markets for your craftwork.

Listings of buyers

Before you take off down the road to sell your goods, compile a list of your target accounts. You can gather names of stores in various ways.

- *Directory of Arts & Crafts Sources* ($14.95) by Warm Snow Publishers, P.O. Box 75, Torreon, NM 87061. Lists gift stores, museum shops, directories of buyers, catalogs and sales representatives looking for crafts.

- A guide that lists store buyers is *The Directory of Craft Stores & Galleries* with over 700 stores, sales reps, craft cooperatives, and mail order catalogs that buy crafts from Front Room Publishers, Box 1541, Clifton, NJ 07015.

- Another listing of more than 1,400 craft buying galleries is *Directory of Wholesale Craft Buyers and Consignors* by Abby Rohrer, 4882 Kings Ridge Blvd., Boulder, CO 80301, (303) 442-2148. They also sell the list preprinted on labels.

- *Gift, Housewares, & Home Textiles, The Salesman's Guide*, ($125), by Reed Reference Publishing, 121 Chanlon, New Providence, NJ, 07974, (800) 223-1797. Listst over 12,000 retail buyers by twenty-five different types like department stores, home shopping TV networks, catalog houses and membership warehouses.

- *The Crafts Reports* has a 'crafts wanted' section where stores buying craft items list what they are looking for and the average price range. There are also ads appearing from mailing list brokers who specialize in craft store buyers.

● To locate buyers in a particular trade, look at Gales's *Directory of Directories* in your library. This reference lists sources of directories like the *Gift Shop Directory* and *Gift and Houseware Buyers Directory.* Also see Appendix B of this book, Buyers Directories.

You probably will spend more money per sale when traveling to get store accounts than you would spend if you were to exhibit at a wholesale trade show. Unless you are producing a large amount of inventory, though, trade shows could result in more orders than you can fill.

In the last few years, the number of retail stores that sell handcrafted items has been steadily increasing. It seems that customers are more accepting of buying fine craftwork when it is displayed in a retail environment; another increase in the number of potential markets you can sell to.

At some point, you must learn how many stores you can comfortably supply. This will depend on how much you want to produce and how willing you are to manage others if you have to hire employees.

Is your work inappropriate for selling in large quantities? One-of-a-kind pieces with lots of detail and finish work are sought after by high priced galleries, but you spend days, maybe weeks, creating one piece. It is difficult to survive by exclusively trying to sell this kind of art because sales are infrequent. The more practical approach is to produce a line of steady selling products, establish a reliable income, and then allot time for working on special one-of-a-kind projects.

Doing wholesale business

The following points will help you analyze your situation and know if selling wholesale is appropriate for you. These suggestions will also serve as guidelines for working with stores.

- The wholesale price you ask will usually be 50% of what the store marks an item. Can you sell to stores and still make a profit? Use the information in Chapter 2 on pricing and figuring profit margins to learn which items will yield a profit at wholesale prices.

- Store owners will tell you what they can and can't move. This means you may be producing to suit their market. Are you willing to work under someone else's guidelines?

- Develop a line of complementary products rather than offering only one or two items in a category. For example, products for the home might include lamps, tables, chest-of-drawers, etc. For clothing, you might make several different kinds of garments. Buyers are more comfortable with a line of several choices. Also, offering a product line conveys an impression of the size and solidity of your operation.

- Store owners want to see consistency of style in your work that distinguishes your pieces from others. Look at the work of successful craftspersons and you'll often see a similarity in design or pattern from piece to piece.

- Some stores insist on exclusivity. They might even want you to sign an agreement that you will not sell your work anywhere else in the same city or area. Avoid such a contract, if possible. It can only limit your sales and there's no reasonable chance that one store will sell any more of your work in exchange for exclusive rights. Alternately, you can use the same situation to get in the door of some stores by promising exclusivity in their region.

- Ask for a purchase order number from a store at the time it places an order. This is especially important with large companies like department store chains where, due to the high volume of merchandise they handle, an order may be refused or questioned. A purchase order is the only proof that they placed an order. Where you have a positive relationship with the owner, there is less likelihood of this happening. Nevertheless, it's best to avoid confusion and protect yourself with a P.O..

- When shipping orders, use United Parcel Service (UPS). Stores must sign for each delivery. This is your record that they received it, in case there's a dispute. It's also easier to track lost packages through UPS than to try to find missing parcels through the postal service. If you do send something parcel post, request a return receipt, though it will add to the cost. Otherwise, there is no record of the package being received.

- Persons or companies ordering goods usually pay shipping charges. Add this amount on to the invoice when billing. Use invoices printed so that 'Freight is F.O.B. (your address)' is clearly seen. F.O.B. means 'freight on board', the point to where you, the seller pays the freight. Some businesses offer free freight to customers who pay for orders in advance.

- Seek store accounts that buy your work outright as opposed to consignment agreements.

- Keep in touch with stores regularly, not only to find out about buying trends, but to also learn what the competition is producing.

- Galleries like copies of your resume handy for customers interested in your work. A well prepared resume will list your education, awards, teaching and speaking credits, organizations you belong to, and previous exhibitions.

Craft malls

Craft malls are large stores that sub-rent small partitioned spaces to individual artisans. Almost all of these jury new work to assure high quality. If the location is good, this kind of arrangement can work well for you because you don't have to be there to mind the store. Artists usually pay a monthly fee and some add a sales commission.

Take the time to check a business out thoroughly, though, before you sign any rental agreements. Visit the location yourself. Ask the manager for the names of other craftspersons participating so you can talk to them about the operation. Find out if other artists are making enough sales to pay the expenses and if the owner pays promptly for crafts sold. It's also important to have your work covered by the store's insurance against fire and burglary.

One organization with over twenty-five craft malls in six states is Coomers Craft Malls, (817) 237-4588. More listings can be found in *The Crafts Report.*

Extending credit

If a store buys your work outright more than once, they will most likely expect you to allow them 30 days to pay for goods received. This is normal terms for almost all businesses. Selling your handcrafted items wholesale may make it more difficult for you to grant credit terms because it restricts your cash flow.

If you can get the stores to pay upon receipt of goods, you won't have collection hassles. Your ability to establish your own terms will be based on how well your work sells. In other words, if your work moves quickly for the store, they are more willing to pay for merchandise up front.

Make your first sale to an account C.O.D. (collecting payment upon delivery). Send the store owner a blank credit application and a request for a financial statement.

You can usually purchase inexpensive blank application forms at your office supply store. Ask for three references. These you should call or write with these questions: What do you make and sell? How long have you been doing business with this store? Do you extend credit terms to them? If so, for how long? Do you recommend this store for credit?

Though many persons strive for integrity in business, some have financial trouble and fall behind in paying their bills. Also, it's unwise to assume that everyone you deal with is honest. A few store owners make it a policy to take advantage of small suppliers.

What happens after you have extended credit and the account does not pay? The more time that goes by on an overdue bill, the less chance you will get your money. After 90 days of being overdue, your likelihood of collecting is 80%, after 180 days your chances drop to 50%.

It's risky to extend credit to stores open for fewer than three years because many businesses fail within the first three to five years of their start-up. Action taken by you in advance is more valuable than any efforts made after a collection problem has come up.

When you are reviewing a credit application for a store, also seek information from Dun & Bradstreet. They collect data on businesses of every size. For information, write Dun & Bradstreet, Dept. 178, 1 Imperial Way, Allentown, PA 18195. To protect yourself from possible collection problems, be on the lookout for:

● Large reorders following prompt payment on small first few orders.

● Reorders sent out before prior invoices are paid.

● Buyers that seem demanding or in a rush.

- Phone numbers not listed with directory assistance.

- Information on credit application that you cannot confirm.

If you do a large wholesale business to the giftware industry, you can screen prospective accounts before you extend them credit through the services of Manufacturers Credit Cooperative of Plano, TX. Member businesses agree to provide a listing of their delinquent accounts to the Cooperative monthly.

Also, members receive a comprehensive listing of reported business's 90-day payment delinquencies, accounts submitted to a collection agency, insufficient funds or dishonored checks, accounts refusing COD orders after ordering, bankruptcy/closings, and other useful information every month.

MCC also offers pre-collection and attorney assisted collection services. Their pre-collection service can be particularly useful in getting payment without arousing animosity. To find out more about their service, write to Manufacturers Credit Cooperative, PO Box 860188, Plano, TX 75086, (214) 422-7852.

Consignment

Consigning your work means that you leave your items at the store without receiving payment until some time after the sale. Pieces remain your property until sold. An agreement with the details of the arrangement is usually signed by the store owner and you.

Consignment is looked on with different feelings by every craftsperson. Some say don't do consignment at all. Others have a softer attitude toward the situation. Almost all consignment arrangements benefit the store or gallery more than they benefit the artist. Stores get inventory at no cost to them. They also have the use of the money from the time of the sales until the time they pay the artist. Commonly, payment is made by the 15th of the following month.

My first wholesale experience was with a retail gallery carrying a variety of craft items on consignment. I was approached by the manager of the shop at a craft show. She seemed enthusiastic about having my work in their store, located on the downtown plaza of Santa Fe where thousands of tourists pass every day. I was too flattered to think that a big retail outlet would be anything but fair and business like.

I left twelve pieces on consignment. One piece sold after the first month. The store did not call me or send a check. I only found out because I had returned to the store six weeks later to see if anything had moved. They wrote me a check while I was there. I briefly wondered *"Would they have paid if I hadn't shown up?"* Another piece was sold soon afterwards. When the agreed time for promised payment went by, I gave the manager a call. She said *"No problem, the check is on the way."* Another two weeks went by with no sign of the check. When I called again, I heard this line *"Oh, sorry, our accountant is out on vacation and she's the only one who can sign the checks."* By then, something started to smell.

I made six or seven calls over the next two months, all long distance, because I lived ninety miles away. It was truly amazing how many different excuses I received for not getting paid. A really good one was *"We're experiencing a slight cash flow problem. It should be straightened out soon."*

When I couldn't sleep one night because I was so angry, I saw the need for stronger action. I called the manager the next morning and said, *"It's been two and a half months since you sold my piece. Every time I call, I hear a different excuse. I'm coming this afternoon to get my money. If you don't have it ready, I'm taking my records of all the transactions to the local magistrate and filing a claim, including all my expenses put out to try to get my money."* When I arrived at the store, they wrote me a check. They acted as if I had hurt their feelings with my accusations.

A few months later, the store went bankrupt, owing several craftspersons for unpaid sales. When I told the story to a potter next to me at a crafts show, he said *"Oh yeah, them. Everybody knows they have a bad reputation for not paying."* This is an excellent example of how talking with

Figure 4.0 Sample consignment agreement

CONSIGNMENT CONTRACT

The undersigned, owner of _____ Gallery agrees that _____ (artist's name) is a consignee of the _____ Gallery, city, state. The medium/media in which the above has been accepted is _____. The artist's work will remain the property of the artist until it is sold. The Gallery maintains an insurance policy against personal property losses, burglary, and liability. The undersigned consignee named in this contract understands and agrees that:

1. The seller shall retain a commission of 40% of list price of any article. The seller shall use the artist's recommended value as a guide for pricing articles.

2. The seller will deduct all consignment commissions from the selling price of any item and will remit the balance to the artist monthly. Checks to artists are written on the 15th of each month for sales through the last day of the previous month.

3. Consigned items will be displayed for 90 days unless the artist is notified otherwise. Upon notification, articles must be picked up within 5 days by the artist or designated agent or they shall become the property of _____ Gallery.

4. The artist does___ or does not___ wish to make articles available through the Gallery's layaway plan.

5. Like works by an artist exhibiting at the Gallery which are for sale elsewhere in_____City shall be priced the same as the established retail price of _____ Gallery.

6. The Gallery requests that a one-week notice be given before removing any items from the Gallery.

7. The _____Gallery retains the right to accept or reject any articles presented by an artist for sale or display and further retains the right to display articles in any manner which it deems appropriate.

8. Items discounted to decorators or designers result in the discount being split between the artist and the Gallery. The amount of the discount will not exceed 10%.

9. The_____Gallery will receive 25% commission on studio sales and all other sales resulting from referral from the Gallery or as a result of exposure of the artist's work in the Gallery.

Articles are accepted by the _____ Gallery for sale subject to the terms and conditions of this contract. The artist specifically represents herself/himself as the lawful owner or agent for the owner of all consigned articles and that there are no liens, encumbrances, or payments due on any article.

This contract will be binding until such time that either party violates the terms of said agreement or until new policies demand adjustments.

_____Signature of gallery owner _____Date

_____Signature of artist _____Date

other craftspersons can help you know ahead of time which stores to avoid.

Are there any good reasons to consign your work? Maybe. One is that some galleries pay the artist 60% of the amount of the sale. This is 10% more than a store buying outright pays for the same piece. You may be asking "Why not raise the wholesale prices to collect the extra 10% when making the outright sale?" If your store accounts will pay the price you want, there's no problem. Every store or gallery I have consigned to has let me set the retail prices. Of course, it makes sense to discuss pricing with the owner to know how similar products are priced. Before consigning your products, consider the following:

● What distance is the store located from you? The farther away, the more chances of problems and the more expensive it is to ship.

● How long has the store been in business? New stores seek work on consignment to fill their displays. They are also the most likely to have problems with cash flow and paying their suppliers.

● Don't consign to stores that buy outright from other craftspersons. Why should you? If your work isn't good enough for them to pay for, there are plenty of other stores that will.

● Ask other craftspersons if the store has a reputation for nonpayment or late payments.

● If you consign, leave at least ten to twelve pieces on display. The more pieces shown, the more you'll sell. You may choose consignment arrangements simply to get in with certain desirable shops. Remember though, you're doing them a favor. If you consign, make it a policy to work with stores where you can generate positive relations with the owners.

Selling on approval

Selling on approval is an alternative to consigning that gives you, the supplier, more of an advantage. In such an agreement, you leave some number of pieces on approval for 60 to 90 days. At the end of that time, if the buyer has made sales, they pay you for those pieces and whatever they decide to keep in the store.

This method lets you test stores as markets without the hassle of tying up inventory for longer periods. If your work doesn't sell, neither you, or the owner will want to continue displaying the pieces.

Sales representatives

If you plan to do a large amount of wholesaling to the giftware trade, you may want to investigate using sales representatives, or reps. Using reps means you can stay home and produce and let them spend the time and expense it takes to show your work to their established accounts. By using several reps, you can extend your exposure to a national audience. They receive a commission from you (15% to 25%) on the wholesale price you are charging the stores. It is important that you figure this cost in beforehand when arriving at a price for work sold to stores. For an example of adding an agent's fee, see page 106, Chapter 6.

Be aware too, reps expect payment from you at the end of the month, whether the store has paid for the order or not.

Supply your reps with brochures, photos of your work, samples, price lists, order blanks, and terms. Make sure you can produce the inventory required to fill the orders coming from more accounts. Know your production limits and keep your agents informed of delivery schedules. Don't expect to receive future orders from a store or a rep when you promise delivery and can't come through.

When considering a sales rep for your products, send the individual agent or company a questionnaire. This is like asking them for their resume, which isn't a bad idea either. Ask for the following information: What other artists do you represent? What is the wholesale price range of your product lines? How long have you been a sales rep (company)? How do you handle refused shipments and canceled orders? What stores do you sell to? What area of the country?

Follow up the references they give you of other craftspersons with a phone call or letter of inquiry asking if they recommend them.

There is always the question of whether the sales rep will actually show your work. They don't have the same time and effort invested in the pieces as you do. You aren't required to sign a lifetime contract with anyone. Typically, a rep will ask for a six to twelve month agreement. If they aren't moving your work, discontinue your arrangement and try someone else.

To find sales representatives for your craft pieces check the *The Rep Registry, P.O. Box 2306, Capistrano Beach, CA 92624, (714) 240-3333*. Another source is the *Directory of Wholesale Reps for Crafts Professionals*, ($15.95) Northwoods Trading Co., 13451 Essex Court, Eden Prairie, MN 55347, (612) 937-5275. This is a comprehensive listing of reps who carry craft items. Also, the classified ads of *The Crafts Report* sometime include listings by reps looking for crafts.

For more information on working with sales representatives see *Working with Wholesale Giftware Reps* ($30) by Jill Ford, Box 2306, Capistrano Beach, CA 92624.

You may prefer to establish new accounts yourself. Talking with owners always gives you insights because they know what sells. Once you decide to sell to stores, the next step in expanding sales is by way of large wholesale trade shows. The following chapter tells you how to find and enter these events and what to expect from them.

Chapter 5
Selling at Wholesale Trade Shows

There are trade shows for almost every industry and interest group. They serve as outlets for the latest trends and designs in products and services provided to any given trade. Each interest group draws buyers and users from all over the country to these events. Attendees include store buyers, interior designers, architects, museum buyers, sales reps and mail order catalog buyers.

When you're ready to expand on a large scale, wholesale shows are the logical means. Before you sign up for one though, you should have a clear picture of what they will require of you. You should also know how big you want your business to grow. A wholesale business requires the inventory, production capacity, and ambition to expand on a national or regional scale. It means deadlines and work schedules, selling at wholesale prices, delays in collecting payments for orders, higher exhibit costs, and hiring help to fill larger orders. It may also mean greater prestige, sense of accomplishment, and increased income.

Large trade shows give you easy access to thousands of buyers. These buyers are keenly aware of what sells and what doesn't in their stores. Talking to them gives invaluable guidance for designing and producing art and craft products. Use trade shows to learn what trends are coming in specific market groups, like interiors or fashion. To reach museum gift stores, for instance, you can get in touch with The Museum Store Association, 501 S Cherry St. #460, Denver, CO 80222, who sponsors an annual convention and publishes a quarterly magazine called the *Museum Store.*

Trade shows make it easy to develop relations with store owners in a friendly, relaxed way. Some of these personal connections can last for many years. Big shows can mean big orders. Many craft exhibitors get enough business from these shows to last all year.

One producer of trade shows for craftspersons is The Rosen Group. The Rosen shows are put on three times a year in Boston, San Francisco, and Philadelphia. The Boston Buyers Market of American Crafts reported average sales of over $11,000 per exhibitor in 1993.

Rosen also sponsors two shows for decorative accessories at the International Home Furnishings Market in High Point, North Carolina. The High Point show draws close to 70,000 buyers.

At these events, you can see what other artists in your medium produce for the wholesale trade. Don't be discouraged by the number of competing exhibitors. The more products you see similar to yours, the greater the likelihood of your success because their presence indicates an existing demand.

Entry requirements

A major determinate in a craftsperson's acceptance in these shows is previous experience as a wholesale supplier. If you apply to them, have the names of stores you have done business with and other wholesale shows where you have exhibited. Producers spend much time and money to put on shows to attract buyers from all over the country.

They expect you to supply accounts on time and in a professional manner.

The Rosen Group Shows offer programs to help new exhibitors wishing to enter the wholesale market. They also offer repeating exhibitors a guaranteed entry without going through the application process. Workshops and seminars are presented on preparing promotional material, display design and wholesale practices.

A publication available from the Rosen Group is *NICHE, The Magazine for Progressive Retailers*. This quarterly magazine is mailed to 20,000 craft and specialty retailers and an additional 5,000 copies are distributed at each of Rosen's shows. Display advertising for craftspersons is available and is a good way to let the buyers know about you before they arrive at the show. *NICHE* Magazine, Drawer 1217, Hunt Valley, MD 21030.

Which trade shows are right for your craft?

Your products can be marketed through several different wholesale trade markets. Craft and gift trade shows can work for many items you make. Fashion shows are a targeted way for marketing clothing and accessories. Interior designers and architects attend trade shows for products used in designing home and office decor.

The major craft trade show promoters are listed in the Appendix. You can also find them in craft periodicals. Write for their schedule and fees. For trade shows by industry, see *Trade Shows Worldwide,* ($169.95), listing 4,500 conventions and trade shows from Gale Research Company in your library. Also, ask to see *Tradeshow Week Data Book,* ($299), by R.R. Bowker, a list of 4,200 international trade shows. Another directory of over 11,000 trade shows is *TradeShows & Exhibits Schedule,* ($170.00), 355 Park Avenue South, New York, NY 10011. Or, contact the Trade Show Bureau, 1660 Lincoln St, #2080, Denver, CO 80264.

It's important that you find the right show for what you're selling. If the show doesn't reach a receptive market for your product, the financial and emotional disappointment could be a serious blow. Research the show carefully. Attend the event in person, talk to past exhibitors, read reviews of the event in trade magazines like *The Crafts Report.* Call the show management. It's in their best interests too that you find the appropriate show for your products. It's worth an exploratory trip to see what happens at these events. Managers are likely to give you a guest pass if you call in advance and explain you wish to attend to evaluate the show.

If you already have wholesale accounts, ask them which shows they attend that might work well for you. What do they look for when they go there? What kind of displays draw their interest? In researching a trade show, find out the following:

- Is this show going to attract the kind of buyers that want your product? How many attend the show? What was last year's sales and attendance? This information should be available from the management when you request an application. If it isn't, call and talk to the manager before you apply.

- How many other exhibitors?

- Does the show coincide with any other large trade show nearby? Sometimes promoters tie their show dates and locations closely to draw more attendees. List all trade show schedules and compare the dates.

- What will be the total cost of doing the show? Booth rental fees on the larger trade shows will cost anywhere from $500 to $2,000 and $100 to $300 more for corner or specific spots. How big is the space? How are cancellations handled? If you ship your display, what will the freight cost?

- What do you get for your money? Is electricity, backdrops, tables, chairs, parking, and unloading fees included in the rental or are they a separate charge? Must union electricians and dock workers be paid for setup? Some exhibition centers in larger cities are run by unions with stringent rules. You can't plug in your own electricity, you must pay a union electrician to do it. If the Teamsters union is in control, you must allow them to load and unload your booth. Unless management lets you carry it in by hand, expect to pay a couple of hundred dollars extra for these 'services'.

- Where is the show held? Is this the first time in a new location? Location changes often affect attendance. How easy is unloading and setting-up?

- Can you produce the inventory to fill large orders? Can you deliver on time? You'll be taking orders to ship at later dates, so it's important that you know in advance the amount of orders you can fill and when you can fill them. Normally some buyers cancel, but you can't know how many. It's better to stop taking orders when you reach your fulfillment level than to promise delivery and then fail to do so. Once you get a reputation for nondelivery of orders, it's hard to regain their confidence.

- Can you afford to sell to large stores that require payment terms of 30 to 60 days? What if an account delays or fails to pay for an even longer time? Can you continue to buy materials, exhibit at shows, and other operating costs?

- Are you willing to hire employees to keep up with the demands of increased production?

● Exhibiting at a major wholesale trade show isn't for the timid. Besides the high cost of booth rental, trade fairs require intense personal stamina and enthusiasm. Demands go far beyond the more relaxed, local art and craft shows.

Advance planning

Trade shows take careful planning, months in advance. As with craft shows, it helps to make a list and check off items as you have them ready.

√ As mentioned before, attend the show before you apply. Talk to the management and other exhibitors about what to expect.

√ Apply for the show early, like six months to a year. This increases your chances of being accepted.

√ Consider advertising in trade publications of the groups interested in your products in advance of the show. *NICHE* is a mixed media publication that goes to craft buyers attending the Rosen Shows. *The Crafts Report* publishes a special show section before each of the bigger shows with advertising available to craftspersons.

√ Send out direct mail letters to previous customers and prospective new accounts. Include reviews and feature articles about yourself. Tell them your booth location and mention new products you'll be showing. Follow up the mailing with phone calls. This method is essential to get buyers to visit your booth.

√ Exhibit center lighting is never enough to effectively show your display. Bring extra lighting, even if you think the hall is well lit. Halogen bulbs create more balanced illumination than incandescent (adds reddish tint) or fluorescent (adds bluish tint) bulbs.

✓   Order tables, chairs, and electricity when you apply. They cost more when ordered at the show. Provide chairs for buyers to sit down, but don't *you* sit if a buyer is in your booth.

✓   Have photo portfolios, catalogs, brochures, price list with terms, business cards, and order forms typeset and printed professionally; allow at least a month for this process.

✓   Make sure your products are tagged, with wholesale prices clearly marked. Display the informational and promotional literature neatly on a small table where you can write orders and hand out your materials.

✓   Have flyers with your booth location mapped out, distributed to buyers when they first enter the show. Also, write your booth number on your business cards and other handouts. Give them to buyers walking through the show, so they can find you again when they return to make their orders.

✓   Buy attractive carpet with padding to cover the floor of your booth. Buyers get sore feet walking on the concrete floors of big exhibit halls.

✓   Arrange travel details in advance, like hotel reservations. Many buyers attending use the hotel designated by the trade show to make contacts after the show hours, though it's more costly than staying in a motel.

✓   Get exhibitor's insurance for the days of the show and transit time to and from to protect yourself from losses or damages. Ask the company you currently use. See Chapter 9 under 'Insurance' for sources.

✓   If you ship your booth, carry some pieces of your work, brochures, order forms, and price lists with you. That way, if your booth display doesn't arrive, you will at least have something to show.

✓   Flameproof your exhibit materials such as table covers and fabric backdrops. Almost all cities have strict regulations enforced by fire marshals inspecting each booth.

✓   Apply for a Dun & Bradstreet number to establish your business reliability. For information, write Dunn & Bradstreet, Dept. 178, 1 Imperial Way, Allentown, PA 18195.

✓   Make an office supply kit including: scissors, tape, staplers, pens, hammer, peg hooks, and anything more you might possibly use at a show.

✓   Consider bringing large pieces of fabric to throw over your display at closing time. Though they wouldn't stop a thief, covers will remove temptation from easy sight.

✓   Make sure the display is sturdy by setting up at home first.

✓   It is to your advantage to know all the rules before you arrive. Show managers provide a regulations and guidelines book for exhibitors. Read it a couple of times and follow instructions to the letter.

Don't hesitate to call the show producers with questions about procedures. Their success is partly based on your success.

Booth displays at trade shows

An average trade show attendee spends as few as thirty seconds at a booth before moving on, so your exhibit has to catch their eye quickly. Displays used for an outdoor craft show will most likely be inappropriate in a trade show. Indoor booths are typically separated by pipe and drape curtains about 3 ft. high on the sides and 8 ft. high in the back. Drapes and pipe are usually provided as part of your booth charge. Buyers should feel free to enter and look at your work. You will make more sales if you build an exhibit that represents how a store or gallery might display the pieces; buyers then have no problem imagining your work in their store.

You can gain useful insights into effective displays by looking at all of the booths in the show, not just the other artists in your medium. Watch to see why some booths attract interest and always have a crowd.

If you feel at a loss for designing a booth and you cannot visit a trade show, many major cities will have 'Display Designers' in the Yellow Pages. Check out their catalogs and floor models for ideas.

If your booth location seems too far from the main stream of browsers, ask the show manager when you first arrive about trading. As in the art and craft shows, there are always last minute cancellations. You can guarantee yourself a better location when you first apply by paying an additional fee for a corner spot. These are the better selling spaces because buyers can see you from two different directions. Prior exhibitors get first pick on locations.

Taking orders at a trade show

Casual conversation is your easiest means of breaking the ice with buyers. After you introduce yourself, ask a question that requires a response to draw them into conversation, like *"What kind of craftwork do you sell in your store?"* If they are wearing a name tag, address them by name.

Ask them about their business. Find out what their needs are. They will tell you if your product will move in their store. Be sure to give them your brochure, business card, price list, order form, and credit application. Do this even with buyers not willing to order at the time.

Thank them for stopping by your booth, shake hands and give them a smile. Many buyers wait till the show is over to place orders. Follow up every lead with a note or phone call expressing pleasure in meeting them and include thanks, even if they didn't place an order.

For more information on doing trade shows, see *How to Get the Most Out of Trade Shows* by Steve Miller, The Adventure of Trade Shows, 33422-30th Avenue S.W., Federal Way, WA 98023.

Chapter 6
Selling to Corporations and Interior Designers

When selling art or craft that has become art, you may find the markets used for selling crafts are too limited. Seeking buyers in the professional business area is a lucrative alternative. Art can take form in wall hangings, tapestries, wood carvings, dimensional sculptures, or many other media.

Purchasers include corporations, hotels, banks, hospitals, law firms, airports, public buildings, museums, foundations, interior designers, individuals, church groups and others. One source mentioned later in this chapter, sells mailing lists of over 650 corporations that buy art.

Corporate opportunities offer large financial returns and new design challenges. You work in large, beautiful spaces where your art will be viewed by hundreds, maybe thousands daily. Your fee is guaranteed by contract, usually with partial payment in advance.

Interior designers are another good market for a craftsperson to begin selling to, because they frequently use local artisans. When you have successfully accomplished smaller projects for them, you find yourself getting more and larger commissions.

It takes hard work to complete a large commission. Corporate commissions involve months of intense effort including research, planning, promotion, financing, contracts, construction of the piece, shipping, and installation. Companies and organizations buy art to beautify what is often, otherwise lifeless space, creating better places to work, play, rest, or pray. Companies also wish to project an image of pride and sophistication through an art piece and give the employees something to relate to besides cold, empty areas. Some companies feel that employees are more motivated by the addition of art to their work environment.

Grants and funding

Grants offer funding for artists to develop their creative work without worrying about paying their bills. Though competition is intense, grants and study fellowships could give you the financial boost you need to get going. A free means of finding out about appropriate funding programs is to call the *Visual Artist Information Hotline,* (800) 232-2789. For no charge, they will send you information on funding sources, insurance, legal assistance, art colonies/residencies, public art programs, and other services for visual artists.

An excellent resource for the crafter is *The Crafters Guide to Grants, Loans and Financing* ($14.95) by Tallman Miller. This resource names grants and programs as well as gives tips for applying. To order, call Craft Business Books at 800-235-6570.

Other resources for available grant funding include:

● The Foundation Center publishes *The Foundation Grants Index* with over 55,000 grant descriptions. They also publish *Foundation Fundamentals: A Guide for Grantseekers* and several other grant resources. For a free catalog, call (800) 424-9836 or write The Foundation Center, 79 Fifth Ave., NY, NY 10003.

- National Endowment for the Arts — request grant program information. National Endowment for the Arts, 1100 Pennsylvania Ave., NW, Room 710, Washington, DC 20506, (202) 682-5448.

- *The Annual Register of Grant Support* by R.R. Bowker, 121 Chanlon Road, New Providence, NJ 07974. Over 1,200 pages of contributions and grants. Check your library.

- *Guide to Corporate Giving* by Robert Porter, American Council for the Arts Books, 1285 Ave. of the Americas, 3rd Flr., NY, NY 10019.

Beyond the financial benefits of winning a grant, the award serves to identify the artist as newsworthy. This helps build a reputation and stimulate demand for the artist's work. Other ways of increasing demand can be accomplished through promotional materials, exhibitions, competitions, teaching, publicity from media coverage, reviews of previous commissions, and advertising.

Promotion for the artist

Promotion is important to a business success. Don't ignore public relations hoping some big name art columnist will discover you and make you famous. An artist's success is more often than not, self-made. Some career advances can be attributed to fortunate detection by the media or generous patronage. But many become known through using some or all of the methods here.

1) **Promotional material:** First, create a portfolio. It should contain a photographic presentation of previous

works, including pictures of at least fifteen to twenty pieces. A resume or vitae conveying a summary of your awards, exhibitions, and education, should accompany the portfolio to provide the reader with written documentation of your accomplishments and contact information. In initial interviews, a photo portfolio is a quick and impressive way to present your work to a project group.

Consider designing high quality brochures as a means of providing a one page summation of your achievements and education, along with one or more photos of your best pieces. The emphasis should be on one or two exceptional works and mention of awards. If you can pick up some brochures of artists at local galleries, they will give you some ideas for designing your own. The successful brochure will include professional ad-quality photos and information on how you can be contacted.

Designers and architects are used to looking at the best quality photo advertising in their search for making purchases. This means your brochure or ad must compete with major home furnishing suppliers who present outstanding brochures. Costs of your promotional materials will not be cheap, but effective promotional material conveys artistic ability and staying power. See Chapter 11 for more ideas.

2) **Exhibitions**: It may take some time to choose the galleries you want to work with. Count on showing twelve to twenty of your pieces many times and talking with several owners. When you and a gallery do decide to work together, they become your agent. A gallery's fee upon selling your work ranges from 30% to 50%. Galleries put on many exhibitions a year to draw customers in to see new works by artists and generate sales. The moment your work appears in a gallery, the show lends you prestige. You must then make use of the flare of public attention to instill your name and work in the minds of prospective customers and

hopefully, art critics. Exhibitions lead to reviews and feature articles, an avenue of promotion explored later.

Exhibition notices appear in the periodicals mentioned below. You can also register as an artist with such groups as those listed in this chapter, your state arts council, museums, galleries, and university art schools. These groups send out mailings of upcoming exhibitions. To find museum exhibitions, see *The Official Museum Directory* by the American Association of Museums, in your library.

3) **Competitions**: Nothing sells like a winning reputation. Competitions stimulate the drive to excel, though submitting your best work to the opinions of others can create tension and frustration. But when you win, that resume just keeps looking better and the dollar value of your work gets bigger and bigger. Better known events offer larger awards and esteem for the winner.

These events are sponsored by organizations that aim to help further the promotion of the art form through increasing contact and information between artist and interested purchasers. Shows, conferences, and competitions are announced in *The Crafts Report, American Craft Magazine, Surface Design Journal, Sculpture, Fiberarts,* and other crafts publications.

4) **Teaching**: Teaching art and craft techniques is a source of building your reputation as an expert while simultaneously supplementing your income. When publications seek newsworthy information, teachers are often sought as a source of reliable verification about techniques and skills.

Teaching opportunities can be found in universities, continuing education departments, art and design schools, museums, and conventions in the media you work with. Institutional positions usually require a degree and some sort of teaching certification. However, if you have written a book on a subject, you can be invited to teach without any certification.

5) **Free publicity:** Another source of promotion is free publicity that comes as a result of reviews and feature articles of your exhibitions by art critics for newspapers or journals. Coverage you receive from a news feature will far surpass what you could purchase through advertising.

It's important to remember to always let the media know where you'll be showing. Whenever you are about to exhibit your work, send a press release to the art editor of newspapers and magazines that review artwork. Many of these publications or listed in the Appendix.

A press release should inform the publication of the who, what, where, when, why, and how of your story. The form should be cleanly typed and double spaced. Use a heading with the name and title of the editor on the first line of the upper left corner all in caps. Follow this with the name of the periodical and then, a short title that tells something concise about your story. Include a release date. Begin the news information about four inches from the top of the page.

Include these elements in the order of their importance to the readers of the publication: who is it about, what is the event, when is it happening, where is the show held, why is it newsworthy. Include any past awards and accomplishments. Make the information clear, concise, and magnetic. At the end, center and type "-end-", then put "For more information, call: (your phone number)."

When you send a press release, write a cover letter to the publication's editor explaining the release briefly. Also, send past reviews or articles about you along with photos of you at work. After a few days, follow up the release with a phone call to the editor to ask if they received it. Don't try to pressure them about whether they will use the information, just ask if they have any questions.

Additional publicity you can seek for yourself is by submitting feature articles about your work to newspapers, newsletters, art periodicals, art and life-style magazines, radio and TV stations. Local newspapers are always looking for feature articles on a 'resident artist of interest' or 'hometown girl/boy' that has done something newsworthy. Sometimes the results can bring dramatic rewards in future business.

To make submissions to newspapers, get in touch with the editor of the life-style or arts and crafts section. You can find out who they are by looking through issues of the paper. Read several of their articles to become familiar with their style. Ask if you can meet them to discuss a feature of interest to their readers. Mention and compliment pieces they have previously written; look up their recent articles to learn their editorial style and the kind of news they write about.

Also, it's important to present the project as a news feature rather than as an attempt at free advertising. Publications want news. Their readers want to find out what's new and worth learning about. Do you have a finished piece you haven't been able to sell? Consider the publicity value when you donate the work to a public building, hospital or community center. Notify the newspapers with a press release!

Magazines are another avenue of free publicity. Publications like *Woman's Day, Better Homes & Gardens, Family Circle,* and *Ladies Home Journal* often feature articles on how crafts are made. Upon your request, they will provide editorial guidelines and schedules. If you have a periodical in mind, write the editor and enclose a SASE, requesting submission guidelines for writers. As with newspapers, you should familiarize yourself with the magazine by reading several recent issues.

Approach magazine editors the same way as newspapers. When you feel you know the style and kind of articles they publish, write an article about yourself and what you do. Call the editor and present the basic information about your work; who would be interested; why they would want to know; what makes your work unique; how they can find the pieces; when the work is available; and how to get in touch with you.

As with the press release, include favorable reviews and awards you have received. If your story has interest to their readers, the editor will tell you. Even if they aren't interested now, their guidelines can help you with future submissions.

You can become known through generating the publicity mentioned in the above techniques. Why pay for something you can get free? When you get in the habit of looking at promotion this way, you will notice other 'free' possibilities as time goes by.

6) **Paid advertising:** A moderately successful artist I know of, was doing well with sales through brokers and galleries. One day he decided to hire a business manager. This person convinced him to start advertising his work in a magazine called *Southwest Art.* His ads consisted of photos of some of his works and his studio address. Interested persons began to call. One piece in the ad was sold to a reader for $10,000. After some months of increased interest in his work, the artist took his work out of the galleries and enlarged his home studio to include a showroom. He told me that even with paying high prices for the ads, he was making 30 to 40% more than he cleared with gallery sales after they took their cut, and sales were increasing, and his name was getting better known.

For the artisan or craftsperson with an advertising budget, consider listing or placing an ad in *Profiles, Who's Who in American Crafts* by the Rosen Group, *The Crafts Report,* or *The Guild* publications from Kraus Sikes, listed on page 103.

7) **Art brokers**: Designers often have direct say-so in commissioning artwork for a corporation. For convenience, they often use brokers in searching for appropriate pieces. Art brokers are familiar with the corporate art purchase process and act as an agent in taking care of the business details. Sometimes galleries also act as agents but may be limited in experience when it comes to commercial art commissions.

One big advantage of having a representative is the relief of dealing with the legalities of contracts. A broker acts as liaison between you and the company, usually earning a percentage of the commission as a fee. Initially, brokers will ask you for a set of slides of your most recent work, a photo portfolio, a vitae or resume, and a list of which of the pieces are available for sale.

A friend who admired some of my wall hangings, told me several times that I should get in touch with his brother-in-law. Maybe I had wax in my ears or something, because despite his repeated insistence, I didn't seem to get the message.

But months later, while I was in New York City, I met the friend again and this time I heard his words, *"Call my brother-in-law. He lives just outside New York. He's a super nice guy. He buys the art for IBM."* HE BUYS THE ART FOR IBM! Why didn't you say so?

When I called the man, he was indeed, very nice. Unfortunately, he had just retired. But, he gave me the names of two of the brokerage services he used frequently while at IBM. Upon contacting them, they asked for twenty slides of my work and prices that allowed for 33% commission to them as brokers.

Sources of corporate buyers

Listings of companies, public agencies and art consultants/brokers that buy or act as agents for artists are found from the following:

● Your state art council or the National Assembly of State Arts Agencies publishes information about public art opportunities and other books. Write them at National Assembly of State Arts Agencies, 1010 Vermont Ave. NW, Suite 920, Washington, DC 20005, (202) 347-6352.

● *ArtNetwork,* 13284 Rices Crossing Rd., Renaissance, CA 95962 (800) 383-0677. Over 30 different mailing lists of artworld professionals including architects, designers, design centers, corporations collecting art, and many more. Average price of each list is $65 per 1,000 names.

● *The Guild: The Architect's Source of Artists and Artisans* Provides list of art consultants and artist reps by state; mural and sculpture artists. 8,000 copies to interior designers, architects, art consultants, and public art agencies. *The Guild: The Designer's Reference Book of Artists*: Includes furniture, rugs, textiles, quilts, fiber, paper, mixed media, accessories, baskets and more. *The Gallery Sourcebook and Buyer's Guide:* Free distribution to 2,000 galleries, museum shops, home furnishing stores and design showrooms. Available from Kraus Sikes, 228 State St., Madison, WI 53703, (800) 969-1556.

● Unique Programs, PO Box 9910, Marina del Rey, CA 90295. Their lists include over 1,000 galleries, 240 competitions, 260 museums and universities, 188 art publishers, 320 corporate collectors, 710 interior designers, 750 architects, 100 department stores and hotels. List prices range from $27 to $45 each.

● *ARTnews International Directory of Corporate Art Collections* (sells list) from Business Committee for the Arts, 1775 Broadway, NY, NY 10019.

● Also, museums, state art councils and similar organizations maintain slide libraries, open to view by purchasers, where you can place slides of your work.

How to get commissions

By using the techniques mentioned above, you put your name and work in the art market to such an extent that brokers, design firms, architects, gallery owners and others know who you are, where you are and what you do. You can call on prospective clients or send letters of introduction along with your resume and photos. Usually, a corporation or organization will have someone in charge of art acquisitions like my friend in New York. This person will often be the public relations director, but could be in the design and planning area.

In any meeting, your past reviews, portfolio or models of previous works will tell the purchaser what they can expect from you. Let them know, in a professional way, what you do and how to contact you when they seek bids on commissioned work. A broker will most likely only present you to their established clients after being assured you can complete the project. Creative ability is only part of what corporate buyers are looking for. They also want a team player, someone with the ability to work as part of a project group involving designers, architects, engineers and management. Purchasers invest in the artist's future success, as much as the work they buy today.

Sizing up the job

Suppose you're commissioned to do a new piece that is not a purchase of an existing work. It's easy to get carried away with the excitement of becoming a recognized and paid artist, but can you do the job? Here are the details you must be capable of handling:

√   There is always a deadline for completion of the work. How closely can you estimate your work time required? Don't be afraid to increase your first estimate. If something can go wrong, it will.

√   Do you have experience in all the skills you need to finish the project, including an understanding of structural needs? If not, can you learn the techniques and materials in the time allowed?

√   Will the materials require flame retarding? How will the colors of the materials be affected by light? How should the piece be maintained through the years? Will the art get natural or artificial lighting?

√   What are the colors of the room; walls, floors, ceiling? Can you work with the project directions of someone who may have artistic senses different from your own?

√   From where in the room will the piece be most often viewed? Viewing distance will affect the finished size.

√   What is the size of the piece? What is the size and shape of the room? What is the design of the architecture, furniture or materials present? Ask the designer for a copy of the blueprints for specifications.

After you know the basic project needs, you are ready to make your proposal. It should include drawings of your ideas, samples of the materials you will use, and possibly a scaled-down model of the piece.

Pricing the art piece

Market value of art work is affected by the reputation of the artist and the state of the general economy. As you grow in experience and reputation, your work's market value also grows. You must consider the cost of a variety of materials like wood, papers, fibers, cane, metallics, or many others. Size of the work and cost of structural support need to be calculated, too.

When quoting prices on a bid, you need a point of reference that accurately reflects your cost of production. Chapter 2 can tell you how to figure the yearly amount it costs you to do business. Remember though, art works increase in value according to the success of the artist.

If you are working through a broker, the commission you pay them should be added to the total price. There is a simple formula for adding the broker's percentage that leaves you the required amount. Say that you want $4,000 for a piece and the agent will receive 33% as commission. You need to find the total amount that subtracting 33% from will leave you with $4,000. Divide the $4,000 by the percentage going to you (100% - 33% = 67%, or .67). $4,000 divided by .67 = $5,970. To check it, simply subtract 33% (.33) of $5,970. This gives you $1,970 for the agent and $4,000 for you.

Draw up a contract covering the details of fees after you have been awarded a commission. Several of the books listed in the Bibliography have examples of artist's contracts. See more near the end of this chapter. Make sure you have added in the time you spent creating a model or sample, meetings with the designers, delivery and installation costs, and agent commissions.

You should receive half the fee in advance to purchase the materials needed. Balance of payment will be due on completion and installation.

Work/study opportunities

If you want to create fine art but have no experience, consider apprenticing with a professional artist studio. This is the best way to gain firsthand working knowledge of how large art pieces are produced, marketed, and installed. To learn of these opportunities, look through the classifieds of current issues of the *The Crafts Report.* They also feature interviews and articles about successful artists and the kind of work they do.

Other sources of openings for artists may be found in: *National Directory of Arts Internships* available from American Council for the Arts. *The Crafts Report* and *Surface Design Journal* often print notices of available positions in large studios. Also try the *National Arts Placement Newsletter*, 1916 Association Dr., Reston, VA 22091, (703) 860-8000. They offer listings of studio artist job openings.

Selling to the interior design market

Interiors is another lucrative market for a craftsperson. Billions of dollars are spent on new construction and remodeling every year. Avenues to this huge industry are opened through interior decorators, architects and interior design trade shows. A large variety of products are suitable for the interiors trade including wall hangings, room dividers or screens, furniture, stained glass, rugs, pillows, throws, sculpture, and more.

Styles always change, providing new opportunities and design challenges for the crafts worker. *Metropolitan Home* magazine explores craft designs for the home. Other magazines like *Architectural Digest* also show trends and can be a source of trendy product ideas.

Retail prices tend to be higher for interiors craftwork. A friend of mine who went to work in her brother-in-law's yacht business in Florida became the designer for the boats' interiors. In this job, she purchased interior fabrics and furnishings from large design studio centers. She told me a handwoven throw about 40" by 72" was purchased from the design center for around $400. The quality of the throw's material was below the level of fabric we were making in New Mexico. For a similar size piece of much better work, we were getting less than $200 retail.

Local designers

Explore your local market by visiting interiors stores, home shows, and open houses, when advertised. This way, you can get a feel for whether you want to work with the style. You can locate names of interior decorators and retail outlets at these events or in the Yellow Pages.

To set up an appointment, go by their showroom or make an introductory call and try to arrange a meeting with the designer to show your portfolio and leave photos or fabric samples. It will help you to keep track of your meetings by building a reference file of every potential customer, including information on the size and kind of business they do.

The first few times you approach a designer or architect, you may feel intimidated by the plush furnishings and elegant surroundings. The more meetings and presentations you make, the more your confidence will grow. Simply walk in, meet the owner, and show them some samples of the work you do. Ask their opinions and what they look for.

The most important fact to remember in approaching this market is *be professional!* Persons working in interiors have sophisticated customers who often spend thousands of dollars to acquire a certain look for their home or office. Interior designers, however, like the advantages of working with local sources. Reliability is the big key here. To establish your credibility, prepare a portfolio of your previous work. Have samples of your work that you can leave with them. You must also know the amount of products you are capable of producing and be ready to deliver the orders when you say you will.

To determine basic pricing guidelines, you can find out what pieces in your area sell for by shopping an interior design showroom. Many medium to large cities have several.

Getting known in the interiors field

The best way to create demand for your work is to build a reputation with a lengthy record of achievements. As in the art world, getting acclaim through winning competitions is an effective tool of self promotion. For example, Hines Interests Ltd. sponsored, along with the American Craft Council, a competition for craftspersons creating for the architectural field. The winning piece was paid a $5,000 purchase award for permanent exhibit. Contests are mentioned in periodicals like *The Crafts Report, Surface Design Journal,* and the other publications mentioned in this chapter. Contest offices will send you an application and guidelines upon request.

Interior design organizations

A large association that can be useful in connecting with the interiors trade is the American Society of Interior Designers (ASID) and another organization, the International Society of Interior Designers. If you can get yourself invited to one of their meetings, you will have the opportunity to meet those in the local interiors field, talk shop and probably receive some good leads. Check your Yellow Pages for members' listings under Interior Designers. Or, write to ASID, 608 Massachusetts Ave. NE, Washington, DC 20002-6006, and International Society of Interior Designers, 433 S. Spring St., Los Angeles, CA 90013. The national headquarters will have information on a branch office nearest you. ASID Industry Foundation (IF) is a group of companies providing products and services to interior designers. IF publishes a member's directory in the June issue of the ASID Report. This directory lists current IF members, their representatives, and products. Advertising space is also available. Write to Industry Foundation, ASID at the mentioned address or call (202) 546-3480.

Interior design trade shows

Interior design buyers can also be reached through regional and national trade shows. This is the best way to keep up with trends in colors, designs and living styles. Attend an interior's show to see what they are about and to get a view of what's currently happening in the market.

Largest of these shows is NEOCON, an exhibition of furnishings, accessories, textiles, and other products for interiors. The International Federation of Interior Architects/Designers World Congress exposition is held jointly with NEOCON in Chicago. For more information, write NEOCON, Suite 470, Merchandise Mart, 222 Merchandise Mart Plaza, Chicago, IL 60654, (312) 527-7600.

The Rosen Group Shows, mentioned earlier in Chapter 5, sponsors exhibitions at the International Home Furnishings Market, aimed at the interiors trade, twice a year at High Point, North Carolina. High Point is considered the furniture center of the world, a good place to gather ideas for trends in products.

Contracts

When working with the interiors trade, businesses that commission art, galleries or brokers, always make use of sales contracts and purchase orders. When you are represented by an agent in corporate commissions, part of their duties is to protect your interests via the proper legal agreements. If you have selected an established agent, they will have the experience with legalities to guide you through the contract process. This can save you money, time, and hassles. You will need a separate contract with them detailing the particulars of their fees and responsibilities.

Whether you work with an agent or on your own, a contract should include specific terms as these:

- Description of the work and how the piece will be constructed.

- When the piece will be completed and delivered.

- How installation will be accomplished and by whom.

- Your fee for the work and when you will be paid.

- Possibility of differences in colors of materials initially chosen due to variations in dye lots.

- Changes in the design or construction of the piece.

- Rights for reproduction.

- Ownership of models. You will want to keep them as examples of your work.

You may at some point consider using a lawyer with experience in legal areas that concern arts and crafts business. If you don't know one with this kind of background, write to Volunteer Lawyers for the Arts, 1 East 53rd Street, 6th Floor, New York, NY 10022, (212) 319-2787. They publish a directory of volunteer lawyers for the arts. Also, see the Bibliography for titles to help educate you on contracts, agreements and other legal issues. Chapter 9 has more on legal advice and resources for craftspersons and artists.

Chapter 7
Building a Mail Order Crafts Business

Mail order offers attractive benefits as a home based business for craftspersons. Orders and payments arrive in the mail, you fill the order and send it to the customer. You do much of your business without leaving home. Success in mail order, or any other marketing effort, comes by targeting the particular groups of customers that want what you are selling. You then focus your time and resources on selling to this group(s).

This may sound simple, but many small businesses waste their small, precious capital resources trying to sell goods to persons who have no proven interest in their product.

Mail order, sometimes known as direct response, is a science, complete with its own statistics and techniques. By following the rules, you can accurately predict in a short time whether doing business by mail is going to work for you. It is important to test a sampling of your target audience with your offer before you spend money on a large campaign. Responses are predictable within a given range. If your ad generates a profit, or at least breaks even, you may decide to 'roll out' with more ads to larger audiences.

There are several methods of marketing through mail order. Only a few media, however, offer a chance of successful response for many craft products. Media most likely to generate sales of these items are 1) direct mail, 2) catalogs offering handcrafted products and 3) magazine ads, display and classified.

Another possibility for selling crafts by mail is through a television home shopping channel like QVC. With an audience of almost 50 million viewers, the participating craftsperson must be ready to ship large quantities of their craft in a secure and timely manner. Additional shopping channels will probably be appearing as more consumers choose to shop from home via the telephone and their credit cards. For more information about selling crafts through QVC, contact GuthyRenker Co., 115 Drummond Dr., Wilmington, DE 19808, (302) 633-1806.

Direct mail

You probably have received several direct mail solicitations yourself. They often consist of a three to four page personal letter promoting a product for sale by mail. In addition, they usually offer a gift, quantity discount, and a money back guarantee. Often, your name is on a list compiled of persons who purchased or asked about specific products.

Companies and mailing list brokers make extra income renting the names of persons who buy their products to other companies wishing to sell to these 'known' purchasers. To find the names of mail list brokers, check the Appendix of any mail order business start-up book in your library. List brokers will send you a catalog of the kinds of lists they rent.

It's difficult, if possible at all, to locate a list of proven retail buyers of particular craft items. You don't need to rent one anyway. Since craft shows draw the persons most likely to buy handcrafted work, you know that almost everyone attending is a potential customer. Start your own in-house mailing list from craft shows customers and others who have previously bought your work. Be sure to include those persons who showed an interest in your craftwork, even if they didn't buy.

Your own list will provide the most profitable source of names. With these names, you can make a direct mail offer of your products that can result in additional sales. Wholesale buyers names can be rented or found from the sources listed in Chapter 4.

An effective way to make such an offer is to write a personal letter to each of your customers. By using a word processing program on a personal computer, you can insert merge codes throughout the letter that will place the customer's name wherever you wish to address them by name. These personal letters get more responses than a standard form offer sent to "Dear Customer."

A good product may not need much help when offered in a direct mail offer. Yet, many parts of a sales offer can be made more effective in motivating the customer to act. To secure the best possible response from an offer, include as many as possible of the following elements:

✓ Stress the benefits of the product to the user. Make it clear why they should buy from you. Capture their interest with this benefit from the beginning of the offer.

✓ Make the letter personal. Use the person's name in the salutation and elsewhere in the letter, if possible. Write in a friendly style without long sentences or paragraphs. **Bold** or <u>underline</u> important points.

✓ Place a time limit on the offer, such as: *'This offer good till November 1st'*. Offer a discount if the order is received before the deadline. Offer a discount for multiple purchases like: *'Buy 4, get 1 free.'*

✓ Guarantee customer satisfaction. Offer to return their money if not totally satisfied with the product. Stand behind your guarantee.

✓ Give the customer the option of paying with a credit card. Make it easy to order with the option of ordering now and being billed later.

✓ Offer a gift for ordering now. For example, a pen with your business name and logo inscribed.

✓ Ask the customer for the order by including an order form and a return envelope to make it easy for them. Tell them exactly how to choose the product they are ordering, how much money to send, where to send it to, and indicate where to fill in their name and address.

✓ Include testimonials of what others have said about your products. Many of your customers will happily allow you to use their satisfied comments in your sales efforts. However, to avoid any legal problems, send them a request for permission with a place for their signature, before you use their words.

✓ Point out details that establish you as a unique and qualified source. What are your credentials? How long have you been a craftsperson? What special techniques or materials do you use?

✓ Add a P.S. at the end of the letter that repeats the chief benefit of your offer or product. Postscripts are the part of your letter most read.

✓ If possible, follow the letter with a phone call. A direct mail offer followed by a personal call has been known to double the normal number of paid responses.

Save advertisements sent to you through the mail and ads that you see in magazines and keep them in a folder. Make this your 'swipe file'. Because mail order is highly competitive, many of the ads you receive will be good examples to emulate.

Check the direct mail pieces sent to you for the items mentioned above. You will find almost all of these offers include many of them.

Direct mail costs

Is direct mail worth the expense? Keep track of the cost of designing and printing your promotional material, your time and the cost to mail it. Add them up. If sales from the mailing generate enough income to pay the expenses and give you a profit, it's worth your while to develop the mail order end of your business.

A ballpark figure for the cost of an average mailing to 1,000 names is between $300 and $400. You can test your product for response and see what happens. If you only break even, you are, at least, generating more name recognition for your business.

If your mailing list contains over 200 names and you foresee mailing more than three or four times a year, you can save money by buying a bulk rate mail permit from the post office. You may need to mail over 750 pieces per year to generate a savings. Annual fee for the permit is around $75. Typical bulk rate in 1994 for a first class letter mailed for $.29, is $.19.

Mail order experts say that you can expect 1% to 3% return on direct mail efforts to a list of names with a general interest in whatever you are trying to sell. Returns can be from 5% to 10% if the offer is mailed to a group that has proven its interest by previous purchase or inquiry. I once received an 11% response from a well produced offer sent to 100 names of proven purchasers. When following up the mailing with another letter and a phone call, the response jumped to 17%.

That's a good response, but did I make a profit? I spent $35 to produce the personal letters, including the cost of the paper. Price of postage was $40. Phone calls came to about $25. Project time involved about 5 hours that I valued at $15 per hour. That's a total cost of $175 for everything. Price of my product was $25 and I sold 17. Cost in producing and shipping the product was $4 per piece. 17 times $4 equals $68. Total income was $425. Total expenses were $243. $425 minus $243 equals a gross profit of $182. So yes, it was worth doing. I have made other offers by mail with much less response and sometimes at a loss. All you can do is test a product, a mailing list(s), and the timing to see what happens.

Catalog sales

Success of catalogs is in part, based on their ability to offer unique items unattainable from another source. Expenses involved in producing a catalog in small quantities make the project infeasible for a small business just starting out. You need several thousand customers willing to buy your products to justify the expense. An alternative is to find existing mail order catalogs carrying similar items. Using the directories mentioned, you can write each company and request their catalog. Once you find the catalogs you want to see your work in, write them a letter of introduction, include your brochure or pictures of your work and your prices. After about a week, follow the letter with a phone call. If the catalog producer decides to accept your work, it is worth discussing their retail pricing experiences with similar items.

You are selling wholesale to the catalog company as you do to a store, usually receiving 50% of the retail price. Be cautious of working with catalog buyers who want a bigger discount off the retail price. A 50% discount is normal and gives you more chance of selling at a profit. You may run into some catalogs that only take products on consignment. If the catalog is new, the chances of it failing are far greater than an established firm and if this happens, you may not be able to retrieve your merchandise.

Many catalogs will drop ship orders. This means they take the orders, either by phone or mail and then send you the quantity, name, and address of the customer along with payment. You ship the product directly to the purchaser.

Products for the home are the most likely candidates for home catalog sales, while shawls and scarves appear in clothing catalogs. Companies that have carried craftwork in the past include *Hearth Song,* 400 Morris Street, Sebastopol, CA 95472, 800-325-2502, *Vermont Country Store,* P.O. Box 1108, Manchester Center, VT 05255, and *Miles Kimball,* 41 W. 8th Avenue, Oshkosh, WI 54906.

Obtain a sample of any catalog before sending your pieces. Ask them how they review new work. You'll know from the catalog whether it's appropriate for your craft. To locate appropriate catalog dealers, see:

- *Directory of Arts & Crafts Sources,* ($14.95), by Warm Snow Publishers, P.O. Box 75, Torreon, NM 87061.

- *Directory of Craft Shops & Galleries,* ($9.95), from The Front Room Publishers, PO Box 1541, Clifton, NJ 07015.

- *The Catalog of Catalogs II,* by Woodbine House, 5615 Fishers Lane, Rockville, MD 20852.

- *Directory of Mail Order Catalogs,* by Grey House Publishing, Pocket Knife Square, Lakeville, CT 06039.

- *The Wholesale-by-Mail Catalog,* by Harper Collins Publishers, 10 E. 53rd St., NY, NY 10022.

Classified ads

Classified ads appear in almost all major magazines toward the end of the publication. Rates, usually by the word, vary according to the circulation. More readers equal higher ad rates. This is true for display ads, also.

It is difficult to generate sales of items priced more than $5 in classified ads. Higher priced products are often marketed in two steps. That is, the classified ad will offer 'free details' and if the reader responds, a direct mail packet is sent to them. This is an inexpensive way of building a mailing list of persons who prove they have an interest in your product.

If you make smaller items like gift boxes, placemats, earrings, pillows, or Christmas ornaments, consider a color brochure with photos and description of products. This brochure, along with a price list and letter about your business could then be sent to persons responding to your ads.

For the craftsperson, newspaper ads to sell products are a waste of money. Because each issue is available daily, the paper is usually glanced through once and then trashed. Magazines, on the other hand, are often kept for months after purchase. I have received responses to ads placed in magazines over four years after the issue when the ad first appeared. The majority of responses, however, will come in the first two months.

Display ads

Display ads are the larger ads appearing throughout a periodical, either with color, or black and white photos. These ads aren't cheap. It is important to know that your advertising dollar will reach an audience who wants your product. A one page, full color ad run one time in a periodical like *Family Circle* may cost about $90,000. They claim over 15 million women readers will see each issue.

Even if you receive enough orders to pay for the ad, can you produce the inventory for thousands of buyers?

Rates drop with black and white ads and for smaller page dimensions. If you want to know a magazine's ad rates, send them a postcard asking for advertising rates and circulation information. They will send you their media kit with a sample issue, rates, layout requirements and reader profiles.

Display ads, in general, should not be placed in magazines where no one else is running ads of similar products. If you see products like yours in such ads, however, check several back issues of that magazine at your library. Advertisements that appear in current issues in periodicals where the ad has run for a year or more, must be getting results. Almost all businesses will cease advertising if there is not enough response to cover expenses.

To learn if a particular magazine is suitable for advertising your product, make a list of groups of consumers that have an interest in your item. Since the largest consumer group in the country is women, women's magazines will be the first place to look. Don't stop your search there, though. Use your imagination and pick up copies of various titles at random, looking through the ads. Check the library for *Reader's Guide to Periodical Literature* and *The Standard Periodical Directory*. You'll find hundreds of subjects and periodicals listed. When searching through these issues, look for other advertisers of craft products like yours.

Words that sell

Advertising is a nasty word to many. It often means misleading the consumer into purchasing something they may not want or need. This belief makes it doubly important to design and word your ads with as much honesty as possible. Also, there are strict laws about misleading advertising. Professionals learn to seduce, not to deceive.

Certain words have proven to be more powerful to influence a reader than other words. Experts employ these words to motivate the public to purchase their products. You can make use of these words too. Among the more effective words are: *new, you, now, riches, bargain, bonus, complete, easy, enjoy, exclusive, fast, free, help, love, proven, save, secret, special, success, today, yes, amazing, compare, power, quick, how-to, important, last chance, magic, startling, why, when, hurry, announcing, improvement.*

Books on the subject of direct marketing and mail order like *Building a Mail Order Business* by William Cohen or John Kremer's *Mail Order Selling Made Easier* will usually list these and other response motivators.

Free publicity

You can achieve more effective coverage than that gained from any kind of advertising by publicity through feature articles. Newspapers and magazines look for newsworthy persons, ideas and events to interest their readers. See Chapter 6 for more about this no-cost promotional method for artists. A news feature tells about where to find you and your products with greater coverage and more reader acceptance than through paid ads and at no expense to you.

Best times for mail offer response

Responses will vary depending on when an offer appears. Certain months of the year yield better results from mail order offers than other months. If you watch your own mail, you'll see more catalogs and offers coming in the first months listed than arriving at any other times. Unfavorable times are in November of an election year, during highly publicized events or national disasters, or in the generally poorer response months at the bottom of the following list.

Here are the months in order of their response success according to many experts. Results of your offer will be better in the months listed first and become progressively slower as you mail at the other times.

Months in order of response from good to worse are: 1) January, 2) February, 3) October, 4) August, 5) November, 6) September, 7) December, 8) March, 9) July, 10) April, 11) May, 12) June.

Repetition of an offer also increases response. One professional advises making seven approaches to a customer over eighteen months. Each offer should be somewhat different to avoid getting trashed immediately. The consistent action of putting your message in front of your customer is more likely to get a response than from making a single attempt. If you don't intend or have the resources to repeat your offer several times in various ways, you may be disappointed in the results.

A note about mail order

A mail order operation for any business should be carefully considered. The advantage is that it's a highly measurable way of doing business. Statistics and laws run true for almost all products marketed by mail. If you want to learn all about direct mail selling, read *Mail Order Selling Made Easier* by John Kremer and *Building a Mail Order Business* by William Cohen. These books offer some of the most useful advice on the subject. They cover everything step-by-step, including lots of examples of product offerings and marketing plans for tracking responses.

Chapter 8
Additional Markets for Arts and Crafts

Religious market

Churches provide selling opportunities for many different craft items. For instance, you will find a market for stained glass windows, woven banners, candles, candle holders, altars, altar coverings, vestibules, tapestries, baskets, urns, wall hangings, and more. To reach the church market, the first step might be your own church or the church of a friend. The organizational arm of the various congregations usually make budget and purchasing decisions. Find out when they meet and ask if you can make a presentation.

In addition, you will also find in many large cities several religious stores that sell a variety of products including crafted items. Visit these retail outlets to determine if your craftwork will fit in.

Almost every denomination sponsors annual conventions like the Southern Baptists Conference. Announcements of these events appear in the publications of the organizations. The organizers of these events often rent space to vendors similar to trade shows. The larger conferences tend to have more vendors exhibiting.

Another way of reaching the religious market is through donation of a piece of work. The donation of such a gift will no doubt be announced at a service. Publicity for you as a craftsperson will bring referrals within the community. You can further capitalize on the event by sending a news release to all local papers, including the church's parent organizational newsletter. This will give you free news coverage that may be more effective than the level of response paid advertising brings.

In addition to publicity, consider submitting feature article information about your craft work to the large circulation church magazines. An excellent reference to what's out there in the way of publications is *The Guide to Religious and Inspirational Magazines,* ($22.95), by Elizabeth Gould and Livia Fiordelisi, by Writer's Resources, 53 Brandon Road, Milton, MA 02186.

Also, these publications may be used for advertising mail order craftwork, especially in the months before Christmas and additional religious holidays.

Selling crafts overseas

After you have penetrated all the markets you can in the United States, consider selling your crafts to buyers in other countries. There are both advantages and disadvantages to exporting. The pros include more sales and selling to markets that may not be dependent on local economic conditions or be filled with competing products. The cons include increased costs like travel, research, accounting and paperwork, longer delays in receiving payments, and ignorance of foreign markets.

To help with these problems, you might make use of Export Trading Companies (ETC) or Export Management Companies (EMC). These are usually small firms that provide market research, appointing distributors or sales representatives, exhibitions at international trade shows, shipping, and documentation. All the producer has to do is fill the orders. Since they have experience in international selling, they understand the requirements for selling overseas. Not all ETCs or EMCs will be interested in craft items. They usually specialize in a limited number of products. There are more than 1,500 ETCs and EMCs in the U.S. A customs brokerage company that has worked with craftspersons in the past is Great Lakes Custom House Brokerage, (716) 874-8870. To identify more companies willing to market your craft products, contact the U.S. Department of Commerce International Trade Administration, Office of ETC Affairs H 1800, Washington, DC 20230 and request information on ETCs.

It is important that you familiarize yourself with the laws dealing with exporting products from the United States. *Basic Guide to Exporting* is available for $8.95 from the Government Printing Office, Superintendent of Documents, Washington, DC 20402.

Possibly, the easiest means of showing your work to overseas markets is The New York International Gift Fair which attracts buyers from around the world. This show is produced by George Little Management, 10 Bank St., Ste. 1200, White Plains, NY 10606, (914) 421-3200. When economic conditions are good, other U.S. promoters also sponsor exhibit areas within shows in countries like Germany and Japan. Check *The Crafts Report* for upcoming listings.

One of the largest merchandise trade shows in the world is Messe Frankfurt held in Germany. With over 4,000 exhibitors from 60 countries, it annually attracts almost 90,000 buyers. Messe Frankfurt can be reached through the German/American Chamber of Commerce, 666 Fifth Avenue, NY, NY 10103 or Messe Frankfurt, GmbH, Ludwig-Erhard Anlage 1, 6000 Frankfurt 1, Germany.

Before entering international trade shows, contact the show producers for guidelines for selling to overseas buyers. See more details on trade shows in Chapter 5.

Selling crafts on university campuses

Some colleges allow craft fairs to be sponsored by their student associations or the university itself. In return, the university takes a percentage of total sales, usually around 15%. The College Blue Book and the Comparative Guide to American Colleges both are directories of national colleges with descriptions of student activities. See your library. For more on selling at craft fairs, see Chapter 3.

Craft products sold as premiums

The premium and incentive business amounts to over $20 billion dollars annually. Products are purchased by businesses for gifts, sweepstakes prizes, publicity and promotions, salesperson incentives, employee performance incentives, tagalongs (given away with sale of another item), referral incentives, and more. Items used as premiums are often purchased in large quantities, but when local businesses look for incentives, they may not need thousands of units.

Companies find incentive products from personal sales calls, at trade shows, and through ads and announcements in trade journals. The major trade shows for this industry are held in Chicago at the National Premium and Incentive Show, 150 Burlington Ave., Clarendon Hills, IL 60514 and in New York City at the Premium Incentive Show, 1515 Broadway, New York, NY 10036. Miller-Freeman, the show producer, also publishes *Business and Incentives Magazine* from the same address.

Additional retail outlets

Retail craft stores aren't the only possible outlets for craftwork. Depending on the kind of craft, it's size, price, fragility, and construction, products can be marketed through a number of alternative retail outlets. For instance:

✓   Gourmet stores stock food and gift baskets.

✓   Children's stores are an avenue for handcrafted dolls, trains, and puzzles.

✓   Airport and hotel gift shops attract travelers in transit.

✓   Museum and hospital gift shops as well.

✓   Gift stores can also be found at marinas in coastal areas.

✓   Beauty shops sometime display jewelry items or let their customers know they have them for sale.

✓   Campgrounds at national parks and tourist areas often sell craft gifts from local artisans.

✓   Christmas shops offer a wide variety of products including crafted wreaths and ornaments.

✓   Fashion boutiques that carry high-end garments are more likely to be interested in handwoven or one-of-a-kind pieces.

✓   Sell clothing and accessories to maternity shops.

✓   Cookware stores are additional outlets for potholders, wood cooking boards, and other kitchen craft items.

✓   Florist shops offer potential for pressed flower gift boxes and related crafts.

✓   A woodworker might sell gun racks to gun stores.

✓   Military bases all have PX's which carry assorted merchandise.

Chapter 9
Basic Business Practices

When you set up of your business, there are basic legal requirements to follow. States and counties will differ as to the exact licenses and fees required, but the general procedure is similar. If you are working from home, you may be able to get by without some of these for awhile. Your home, however, may not be zoned for business operations. If you are quiet about what you are doing, no one may ever bother you. But, if an antagonistic neighbor or official gets wind of your activity, you could legally be shut down.

Permits and licenses

If your business operates under any name other than your own name, you must file for a fictitious name statement. This is also known as DBA or 'doing business as'. If you want to use a fictitious name for your business, apply at your county clerk's office. They will tell you the fees and application process.

Part of the procedure may involve publishing your intention to use the name you plan to do business under in a local newspaper, usually for a period of two to four weeks.

You will also be required to get a local business license. This is a yearly permit to do business in the county or city where you will be operating. When you apply for the fictitious name statement, ask the county clerk for a business license application.

State sales tax

Almost all states levy a tax on products, and some services, sold in the state. You are required to collect and pay a tax on each sale that you make. Usually, the state sends you forms to fill out and return with payments monthly, quarterly, or yearly. Almost all states require a sales tax permit or resale number from every business that sells products. Sometimes the state will require a deposit from you as guarantee. You may convince them to grant you a temporary permit not requiring a deposit by presenting yourself as a part-time craftsperson doing only one or two shows. You can renew the permit if your business grows. Apply at your state taxation and revenue office. As mentioned in Chapter 3, some craft show producers include the necessary information in their application procedure.

Federal identification number

For taxes, the federal government requires you use either your Social Security number or a Federal Employer Identification Number. If you do not have employees, you can use your Social Security number. Corporations and partnerships, along with employers must get a federal identification number.

Legal forms of business

You must choose the legal form you wish to operate under. There are three legal forms that your business can take: 1) a sole proprietorship, 2) a partnership, or 3) a corporation or S-corporation.

Sole proprietorship means that you are the sole owner. You own the business, manage the finances, pay the taxes, and are responsible for the debts. Every business, including sole proprietors, pay estimated income taxes four times a year. In a sole proprietorship, you are responsible for the obligations of the business. In the event that damage claims are brought against your company, your personal assets, that is money and possessions, can be seized to satisfy them. Many small business owners incorporate their company to protect their personal property from this liability. Sole proprietorship is the easiest kind of business to set up and involves less paperwork than in a partnership or corporation.

A **partnership** means that two or more persons jointly own the business. Each partner is legally responsible for the financial debts and obligations of the partnership. This means that all partners can be held liable for actions taken by any other partner doing business under the company name. For example, if one partner borrowed money for the business, the other partners are equally responsible whether they knew about the loan or not.

Possible legal complications of a partnership business make the head spin. If one partner dies, their spouse may inherit that half of the business. Who makes the final decisions when conflicts arise? What happens if one partner wants to get out? If you are considering a partnership with someone in a business, imagine that you are getting married to them. It takes the same hard work and compatible personalities to make either a success.

A **corporation** is a business whose owner(s) are shareholders of the company's stock. The business is considered a separate entity from the owners, which means that owners, in general, are not liable for the debts and obligations of the corporation. There is also some measure of liability protection for the owners in lawsuits against the company. A corporation's profits are double taxed. This means that the corporation pays income tax on year end profits and then when dividends are paid to the shareholders, they pay income tax on these profits again.

There is more paper work involved with a corporation than in any other form of business. The owner(s) can be hired as employees; that means their wages are an expense, deductible from the corporate income. Any other benefits given to the owner/employee like insurance and paid vacations are also legitimate tax deductions.

Another form is called the **S corporation**. Its form is similar except that the corporation itself does not pay income tax. Shareholders still pay tax on income from dividends.

Of the three forms of business mentioned, the sole proprietorship is probably the most suitable for starting a small business. If you open a retail store or your income from the business exceeds $25,000 a year, then incorporating might give you the advantages of liability protection and the tax deductions of your salary and benefits as a corporate expense. If you have doubts about your situation, consult a Certified Public Accountant for an analysis of what form your business should take.

When you have established yourself as a legal business, there are different systems you can use to keep track of where your money is going. The method you choose should be convenient and give you access to facts about your operation whenever you need them.

Raising money

How will you cover the costs of starting or expanding your business? You will need money for show rental fees, travel expenses, additional raw materials to replace what you use, office supplies, photography, and production costs of promotional material like business cards, brochures, and price lists.

You might want a computer or advanced equipment that is faster and more effective for executing your design ideas. Increased sales could mean hiring someone to work for you and larger and more frequent material purchases. You might want to do more shows and need capital for advance rental fees. These possibilities include only a few of the situations that arise in an expanding business.

Capital for your business could come from several different channels. Your own savings is the most likely source. Other possibilities are friends and relatives, personal credit cards, a business loan through your bank, a personal loan from your credit union, microenterprise programs, and grant funding from national, state, or corporate programs.

Borrowing from friends or relatives

Friends might be willing to lend you money for your needs. Unless you are ready to risk their alienation if something goes wrong, it might be safer to ask them to co-sign a loan made through the bank. Your friend will still be liable if you fail to repay the loan. But if you are confident the opportunity for realizing greater profit is a good one, explain your plan in depth. Show them your business plan with all the actions you will take to increase sales and income to repay the loan. If you keep it on a business level, they will pick up on your confidence and your chances of getting their help and keeping their friendship improve.

Personal credit cards

There is probably no easier means of getting cash or make purchases than by using your own credit cards. With Mastercard, Visa or American Express, you can make cash advances at almost all banks for any amount of your available credit on the card. The money is available by your signature alone. Unfortunately, interest rates on credit cards are higher than almost any other lending source. If you don't repay the loans promptly, interest adds up quickly.

When traveling to make sales calls or to do craft shows, a credit card can handle almost any emergency repairs that occur with your car. You can also pay for motels and food without having to carry lots of cash. Again though, pay off the total each statement or you'll soon find yourself owing more in interest than you could possibly find is worth the convenience of having the cards.

If you don't have credit cards or a credit history, there are a couple of ways to get them. Your bank will issue you a card if you agree to assign your savings as collateral to the amount of your credit limit. In other words, they love to lend you your own money and charge you interest for using it. After some time has passed and you have proved you're a good credit risk, your collateral will be released.

Another method of acquiring cards is to apply first to the major oil companies like Shamrock, Exxon, Shell, Phillips 66 or others. Their requirements are less stringent and many of them will issue you a card quickly. Once you have established credit by making purchases and paying them off, then apply for the cards like Mastercard, Visa and American Express.

You're much more likely to get a credit card if you have a job or have an established source of income. So, if you are working now, get as much established credit as you can before embarking on your business.

Bank loans

Though credit cards are essentially bank loans, you can also apply directly to your bank for cash loans. Again, it is easier to get a loan once you have established credit by paying off previous loans. But even if you have, they will usually ask for collateral on a loan or a co-signer with good credit. Money lenders who review business loan applications of any kind will want to see a business plan. If you foresee seeking loans for your business, you will need to draft a detailed plan as described in the next chapter.

Financial institutions that make loans want confirmation that there is a demand for your craft products. This could be in the form of sales reports and letters from satisfied customers. Lenders care more about the marketability of your products than in the product's novelty. They also want to know how the loan can generate enough extra business to pay back the money.

SBA loans

If your bank turns you down, another option is convincing the Small Business Administration (SBA) to back your loan. SBA does not usually make direct loans. It does guarantee from 75% to 90% of a loan, working through your bank. The SBA will not consider your application until you have been rejected by a bank. As when applying for bank loans, you must convince them your plan will work. Show them your ideas in the form of a business plan and explain how you will carry them out. For a more detailed look at the process, see *SBA Loans; A Step by Step Guide* by Patrick D. O'Hara.

Beyond lending money, your local SBA office is a great source for information on starting and running a business. They provide a series of how-to publications covering accounting, financing, pricing, management, and many other topics.

Another help program usually found in the same offices as SBA is run by the Service Corps Of Retired Executives (SCORE). Here you will find retired executives who volunteer their experience in advising small new companies. They offer free and low-cost training in all the basics of running a business.

Small Business Institutes (SBI's) are sponsored through the SBA on over 500 university and college campuses. Management counseling is provided by students at senior or graduate levels in the business administration programs under faculty supervision. Visit a SBA office near you to find out more. Many major cities have a branch listed in the government pages of the phone book. Or call (800) 827-5722 for any information on the above services.

Microenterprise programs

These programs are usually local groups of craft and small businesses who meet regularly to learn about each other's business and give advice. Members submit loan proposals to a group council which then makes a decision to grant the loan. The funding for the loans comes from government or private sources like the Ford Foundation and the SBA.

These programs also require the borrowing member to take courses in business skills. For sources of these programs, see Directory of Microenterprise Programs, ($10), from Aspen Institute Publications, Box 222, Queenstown, MD 21658 and also contact the Association for Enterprise Opportunity, (312) 357-0177, an organization that advises low-income entrepreneurs.

Credit unions

Credit unions are more friendly, assuming you are a member, but may not make you a business loan. Lending policies for members are less stringent than that of banks. Credit unions are created to help the member/owners. You can become a member of one usually through association with a specific interest group like a cooperative or as an employee of some field of education. When you seek a loan, say the money is for a vacation. Just don't take one, yet.

Additional funding sources

Grants are available for artists and craftspersons to develop their careers without the worry of paying bills. Sometimes the money given may be used to begin or expand the business end of an artist's work. See unding sources listed in Chapter 6.

As mentioned before, *The Crafters Guide to Grants, Loans and Financing* ($14.95) by Tallman Miller is a complete resource for grants and other programs for the professional crafter. The book also provides tips for applying and how to write proposals. To order by credit card, call Craft Business Books at 800-235-6570.

In addition, several books that list different money sources for craft and other new small businesses are:

√   *Directory of SBA's Small Business Investment Companies,* call (202) 205-7589.

√   *Money For Visual Artists,* edited by Suzanne Niemwyer.

√   *Free Money for Small Businesses & Entrepreneurs,* by Laurie Blum.

√   *Government Giveaways for Entrepreneurs,* by Matthew Lesko, from Craft Business Books, 800-235-6570.

√   *Money Sources for Small Businesses,* by William Allarid.

Bartering for services

Another option for paying for essential services is through bartering or trading. I was at the local printer's shop one day ordering a large quantity of printing work when I overheard the owner talking to someone else about trading services. I asked if he'd be interested in swapping my print job for something I could make and he agreed to it. My printing bill would have been $375; instead I spent two days creating his family a queen size, handwoven throw. A rug weaving friend of mine traded his rugs for several hundred dollars in dental work.

Keeping records

Record your sales and production to an inventory record like the one in Figure 9.0. This form is to track quantities of each item you make. You should keep separate lists of a) finished pieces, b) materials used in construction, and c) all equipment used in your business, including tools,

Figure 9.0 Sample of inventory record

INVENTORY OF CRAFT ITEM: Pillow				
DATE OF SALE/ENTRY	MARKET	ITEMS MADE	ITEMS SOLD	WHAT'S LEFT
3/30				23
4/1		20		43
4/20	store order		36	7
4/30		24		31
5/5	craft show		12	19

light fixtures, computers, and so on. There are several good reasons for doing this.

- An inventory of your finished, ready-to-sell goods is essential. By knowing how much stock you have, you can estimate the number of shows you can do and how many store orders you can fill. You can track sales of particular items, styles, colors, designs, and contents to know what's selling and what's not.

- Any materials going into the production of a product are usually considered an expense deducted from the income of the sale, but only when the item is sold. Inventory of raw materials and finished pieces not yet sold are all assets of your business, not deductible expenses.

- Equipment bought and used for your business can be depreciated over time, allowing you to deduct a percentage of the expense over a few years. Time periods and percentages change, so check with an accountant or tax guide book for more details. By keeping an inventory of your equipment purchases, including improvements and repairs, you will be in an excellent position to get the full amount of deductions allowed by the tax laws.

- Another excellent reason for keeping complete inventory records is to provide proof of value in the event you must make an insurance claim. Keep duplicates of your updated inventory records in a safe place like a safety deposit box at your bank.

Keeping inventory is just one of the essential recordkeeping habits you should adopt. If you set up an organized system for your records from the time you start business, you'll save countless hours of searching for important information and you can make instant decisions with the facts right in front of you.

As a business, you're legally required to keep records, including receipts of sales. Receipts for expenditures provide proof of legal deductions from income for tax purposes. As a business, you are always subject to the possibility of a tax audit by the IRS. Prepare yourself. Follow a good record keeping plan and store your records safely. Keep all of your receipts for the last five years or longer. Beyond the legal requirements, it's inevitable that situations arise when you need to look up information from a previous year.

Keeping records is easy. Buy an inexpensive plastic file box from an office supply store. Using file folders, set up files for your sales, each of your expense categories, bank statements, address lists, show applications, and so on. Every time you buy something for business purposes, put the receipt in its proper file. Be sure to write on the receipt, if it isn't clear, what the expense was for. Your basic record keeping will come under these categories:

- A filing system such as the one just mentioned.

- Your business checkbook.

- Sales receipts and sales reports.

- Inventory listings of finished products, equipment, and raw materials.

- Accounts payable and receivable. That is, money you owe and what's owed to you.

- General ledger for tracking daily transactions.

- Travel and entertainment expenses log. Figure 9.1 shows an example of expenses and reasons for business trips.

Figure 9.1 Travel and entertainment log

TRAVEL & ENTERTAINMENT LOG				
DATE	LOCATION	REASON	CLIENT	COST
3/15	Harvest Cafe, Denver	dinner	Mrs. Brown, store owner	38.5
4/7	Kelley Restaurant, Phoenix	lunch	show	12.76
4/7	Motel 8	overnite	show	28.98

Figure 9.2 Telephone log

BUSINESS CALLS TELEPHONE LOG						
Date	Time	Number called	Name of business	Reason	Length of call	Billed amount
2/13	10 am	303 123-4567	Brown Gallery	set appt.	5 min.	4.38
2/14	8:30 am	505 765-4321	Office Max	check hours	.5 min	0.35
2/14	9:15 am	505 567-1234	Tree Gallery	sales call	12 min.	3.99
2/15	5:10 pm	602 666-6666	Powell Shows	check available booths	4 min.	2.56

You can track your business phone calls in the same manner. Make a log like the one in Figure 9.2 to record long distant phone calls by date, time, and number for keeping track of expenses and to refer back to when needed.

Some of the other business expenses you are allowed to deduct include insurance, show rental fees, bank charges, trade periodicals, advertising, office supplies, utilities, contract labor, salaries, equipment rentals or repairs, depreciation, and the cost of goods sold. While on a business trip, save all motel and restaurant receipts, toll and parking fees. IRS provides free publications outlining guidelines for taxpayers. Call (800) 424-3676 to order Publication 910, *Guide to Free Tax Services*. 910 lists the publications you may need for a business.

A sample ledger for tracking expenses is on the following page in Figure 9.3. Workbooks for recording daily transactions can be found at office supply stores and many bookstores. Two excellent guides to records keeping and operating a small business are *Small Time Operator* by Barnard Kamaroff and *Recordkeeping, The Secret to Growth and Profit* by Linda Pinson and Jerry Jinnett.

Ask other craftspersons which accountants they use. Try to locate a professional who has experience in arts and crafts businesses. For more information on getting low cost accounting advice, write to the Accountants for the Public Interest, 1012 14th St. NW, Suite 906, Washington, DC 20005.

API is a national nonprofit organization whose purpose is to encourage accountants to volunteer their time and expertise to nonprofits, small businesses, and individuals who need low-cost professional accounting services. Work is carried out by a growing network of affiliates and more than 4,000 volunteers across the country.

Creating a logbook

Another useful record is a production logbook. A logbook will have a picture of each piece or style with details of material costs, production time, drafts, assembly instructions, and notes about the work. A log can save you design and layout time when you're planning your schedule.

Figure 9.3 Weekly expense ledger

EXPENSES							
Acct #	Account	Total this week		Total up to week		Total to date	
1	Mdse/materials	38	85	38	85	38	85
2	Accounting						
3	Advertising			142	60	142	60
4	Auto expense	24	13	376	84	400	97
5	Electricity			213	22	213	22
6	Freight	12	34	42	71	55	5
7	Insurance			119	87	119	87
8	Interest	2	34	54	22	56	56
9	Laundry			9	18	9	18
10	Licenses			36	OO	36	OO
11	Misc. expenses	4	433	17	77	22	20
12	Office			24	48	24	48
13	Postage	11	OO	23	12	34	12
14	Rent			678	55	678	55
15	Repairs						
16	Telephone			78	9O	78	9O
17	Trade dues						
	SUB TOTAL	93	9O	1177	22	1271	12
	TOTAL THIS WEEK	93	9O				
	TOTAL UP TO THIS WEEK			1177	22		
	TOTAL TO DATE					1271	12

Figure 9.4 Photo log/journal example

Photo or sketch:

Title and Project Description:

Materials & Accessories:

Assembly Instructions:

Finishing:

Total Labor Hours and Costs:

Materials Used:

Total Cost of Materials:

Total Production Cost:

Retail Price:

Net Profit:

Notes:

It can also remind you of previous works that should be kept in production. See the example of Figure 9.4 on page 143.

Insurance

At first, you may not want to add another monthly bill like insurance to the cost of staying in business. Insurance does give you a certain peace of mind though, if you have a large inventory of materials, finished goods, and various pieces of equipment.

If you have children or dependents that will suffer financially from your having an accident, insurance coverage could save you and them hardship. You might need coverage for worker's compensation, fire, flood, theft, and liability. If you rent studio or business space, insurance may be required in the lease.

If you do decide to insure, the coverage should be for the actual buildings that you work or sell in; your inventory of crafts, including when you take them to shows; equipment, tools, and furniture; and for loss of earnings in the event of an emergency that interrupts normal business.

Employee injuries on the job can open you up to legal action. Employers are required in almost all states to provide worker's compensation insurance. This is an expense an employer cannot legally avoid. If employees will be working from their own homes, workers compensation insurance rates will be more than twice the normal amount. They view home employees as high-risk. It will be easy for the worker at home all day to claim any injury as work related. If you hire employees or contractors, adopt safety measures for all aspects of the work environment.

To learn more about health insurance for craftspersons, see *Health Insurance: A Guide for Artists, Consultants, and Other Self-Employed,* ($15.95.), by Lenore Janecek, from American Council for the Arts, (800) 321-4510.

For information on safety issues for craftspersons, write to *ACTS Facts, the newsletter for Arts, Crafts and Theater Safety* at ACTS, 181 Thompson St., #23, New York, NY 10012, (212) 777-0062.

Visual Artists Information Hotline 1-800-232-2789 will send you the names of artist organizations whose members are offered group and special insurance coverage.

In the event you should have to file a claim, the following will help increase your chances of getting paid:

✓ Read the policy carefully. Make sure the policy and the insurance agent are clear about what will be covered.

✓ Be sure to inform the insurer of all equipment you use in your business.

✓ Notify your agent immediately when there is a loss.

✓ Make a thorough inventory of equipment and products according to costs. Save your receipts. Send a copy to the insurance agent. Take a videotape or photos of everything covered and update whenever you purchase more.

Consider complete auto insurance coverage, including towing coverage. Membership in auto clubs like AAA (American Automobile Association) or NMC (National Motor Club) offer a variety of benefits like towing, locksmith services, quickest route maps, and life insurance options. AAA usually has branch offices in major cities. Write to NMC at National Motor Club, 2711 Cedar Springs Rd., Dallas, TX 75201.

Employees

A one-person business is easier to manage than a shop with employees. When you hire workers, you spend much of your time preparing their work, training them in your techniques and correcting their mistakes. They won't do the quality of work you will. And the possibility is good that one day, a smart employee will take the knowledge they gained from working for you, plus some of your design ideas, and open a competing business.

Bureaucracy doesn't help the employer either. Our government has a mountain of paper work to add to your already crowded schedule. Whatever you pay a worker, figure in an additional 30% to cover the social security payments, unemployment insurance, and worker's compensation insurance that employers must pay. Then add in the extra hours for accounting and record keeping to keep it all straight.

As sales grow, you may find yourself faced with the decision to use outside help. You become so busy that you need help to produce your products. You have two basic options — one, to hire employees and the other, to use independent contractors. You can avoid the extra paper work and payroll expenses of being an employer by hiring contractors who are paid flat fee per piece or project completed. They take care of their own tax withholding and worker's compensation insurance. Of the different payment methods you could arrange, it's easier for you to pay for work by the piece, because you spend less time accounting employee transactions and you know clearly what your profit margin is in production costs.

Many businesses have been fined for hiring workers as contractors when the government later steps in and says they were really employees. IRS can assess you back payroll taxes that you had not counted on paying. This redefinition process by the government is on the increase.

The IRS has a list of twenty factors it looks at when assessing what an independent contractor is. If the contractor you use is performing their service to more than one business, has their own tools or equipment, is free to set their own hours and to hire their own assistants, and operating out of their own home or office, they will probably be looked upon as a legitimate contractor. If they work only for you and at your facility, the government considers them an employee.

It is important that you identify the classification to avoid possible fines and back payroll taxes. IRS publishes *Circular E-Employer's Tax Guide,* a free set of legal guidelines and definitions, call (800) 424-3676. For businesses regularly using contract labor, consider the newsletter *The Independent Contractor Report.* It provides up-to-date information on legal cases and other topics about contractors. A free sample is available from *The Independent Contractor Report,* James Urquhart III Seminars, 2061 Business Center Dr., Suite 112, Irvine, CA 92715. Another source of information on the legalities of contractor relationships is *Independent Contractor Contracts: Sample Provisions and Contractor Descriptions,* published by Volunteer Lawyers for the Arts. To order, write Volunteer Lawyers for the Arts, 1 East 53 St., 6th Flr., NY, NY 10022..

If the growth of your business requires hiring help, the biggest question in your mind probably should be whether you want to spend your time managing others and doing more paper work, or creating and selling.

Licensing your designs

Artists, craftspersons, and designers can grant the rights to reproduce their works for specific markets and periods through licensing agreements. In exchange, the designer will receive a fee or a combination of fee plus royalties on sales. In licensing your unique patterns to major companies, you increase your reputation as well as your income.

The International Licensing Industry Merchandisers Association is a trade organization for this industry. They put on an annual trade show where corporate, fashion, lifestyle, and other design properties are exhibited. The show provides a chance to showcase and review new designs. For more information, write LIMA, 350 Fifth Avenue, Suite 6210, New York, NY 10118, (212) 244-1944.

A licensing agreement must cover many details of the artist/company arrangement. How will the royalties be determined? Will the designer receive a flat fee for the use of the design or an advance against future sales? Is the licensing agreement to cover a specific product usage or territory?

To find out more about how to negotiate a licensing agreement, read *Licensing Art and Design* by Caryn Leland. She shows how ideas and images can be turned into profitable business ventures through licensing. She also covers copyright, patent, and trademark laws; explanation of a licensing agreement; strategies for negotiation; example agreements for licensing, agents, and the protection of ideas; and lists of trade shows and publications to help find manufacturers seeking designs.

Sources of legal advice

You probably won't need legal services when you first start your business. After time though, situations will arise that require some form of legal negotiation or documentation. One example is a contract between yourself and a business commissioning you for a project. Before you pay for an attorney's services, familiarize yourself with the information in the books listed following. If, afterwards you feel you are over your head in the complications, then consult an attorney. To locate an appropriate attorney, check with Volunteer Lawyers for the Arts, listed on the previous page. They publish a directory of their members who volunteer or offer low cost legal advice for artists who cannot afford a lawyer. The following resources provide sample legal agreements of use to craftspersons:

- *Making it Legal: A Law Primer for Authors, Artists and Craftspeople* by Martha Blue.

- *Business and Legal Forms for Fine Artists* by Tad Crawford.

- *Legal Guide for the Visual Artist* by Tad Crawford.

- *The Artist's Friendly Legal Guide* by North Light Books.

- *Business Forms and Contracts in Plain English for Craftspeople* by Leonard DuBoff.

Stay up-to-date

Get current news, marketing advice, networking contacts, and reviews to help you keep up with trends and changes in laws that affect home based businesses. *Barbara Brabec's Self-Employment Survival Letter,* P.O. Box 2137, Naperville, IL 60565 is issued six times a year. Every issue provides helpful tips that can save or make back much more than the cost of the subscription.

A superior guide for new business owners has been written by Bernard Kamaroff, C.P.A., titled *Small Time Operator: How To Start Your Own Business, Keep Your Books, Pay Your Taxes, And Stay Out Of Trouble.* This manual contains all the details of setting up a business from scratch. There are many charts and examples of record keeping, profit/loss statement, inventory, taxes, and how to deal with the IRS. It's written in plain language anyone could understand and benefit from. Even if you don't intend to do your own taxes, it's important that you familiarize yourself with all the possible deductions allowed by the IRS.

Chapter 10
Writing a Business Plan

Why are you in business for yourself? You have hopes to gain financial independence, a greater sense of esteem, the freedom to spend your time as you will, and to find avenues that allow you to pursue creative endeavors. To achieve your needs, it's important that you have a clear picture of what your business is all about and to concentrate your energy and resources in effective actions. Four out of five small businesses fail within the first five years, usually because of a lack of planning or sufficient capital.

If your thoughts are vague about what you want, writing them down may clarify your thinking. Sometimes the things we really want are obscured by surface thoughts. Writing will help you focus, organize, and learn about what you want.

You may resist the idea of preparing a plan because you think *"I have better things to do that are more impor-tant."* Without a focus, however, your production and marketing efforts tend to go any old which way, losing impact and costing you time and money. When you start out and even as you expand, you are moving into territories you know little, or nothing about. Yet somehow, you need to find or make a road map of how to get there. Think of it in the same way you accomplish any craft project. When you draft your designs and patterns for a product, you are making a plan for how you will produce the item. First, you have the idea. Then, you sketch it out. Next, you assemble your materials, or resources. Finally, you do the action of making the piece. A business plan can be thought of in the same way.

Many business guides advise creating a detailed plan of long term goals for the next three to five years. Realistically though, how do you know, when you're just starting, where you will be next year, much less in five? As a craftsperson, you may not need a multi-page, comprehensive business plan until you approach a lender for borrowing money for business expansion.

A plan does not have to be elaborate, long term, permanent, restricting or tedious. It can be as simple as jotting down your notes and arranging them clearly. Simplest of business plans is an organized list of your ideas for how you will sell your products like in Figure 1.2 on page 24. The important thing is to get the thoughts down on paper. Keep them in a notebook or file folders. Divide them into topics like products to make, markets to sell to, promotional material and so on. Then list projects that should be attended to in the order of their importance. Using the information in previous chapters, you can draft an effective priorities schedule like the one presented later in this chapter.

Make planning and organizing a habit and you will accomplish more with your time. As your business grows, it becomes increasingly more difficult to remember important ideas that slip from memory. Without a plan, you find yourself attempting a hundred different tasks, instead of focusing on the most important one in front of you. A plan can be for next month, for six months, or for two years or more. You can change it at any point. You can write it in simple words that say exactly what you mean. It's the

focusing and organizing process, just as in accomplishing
any crafts project, that is important. No, not just important,
ESSENTIAL!

Change your plan whenever you get new information
about markets, production methods, or your personal goals.
You can believe changes *will* happen. Opportunities are
found in every situation. Stay flexible and you'll increase the
likelihood of prospering from the unexpected. A plan is a
tool, not a religion. Experiences teach you more about your
business as you go along.

Elements of a business plan

A comprehensive business plan is needed when you
seek loans or credit extensions. Typically, a plan is divided
into four or five sections including:

1) A title page with your company name, address, phone,
trademark or logo, owners' names, date of the plan and
the author.

2) Statement summarizing the purpose of your business.
This can be two or three paragraphs telling briefly about
your business, where it is located, how long you've been
open, the reasons you are seeking a loan, how you will
use the loan to bring in more business, how you intend
to repay the loan, and the size of your own financial
investment.

3) A complete description of your business containing
information on the products you produce, how they are
made, cost of materials, labor and production, and how
you reach your customers. You should also list your
qualifications, employees, accounting methods, and
insurance coverage. This part of your plan needs to show
real figures.

4) Marketing plan that includes the different groups, like those mentioned in Chapter 1, who buy your products, how you reach them, how a loan will help you sell more products, how much and what kind of advertising you do, who is your competition, what makes your products unique, your previous experience and knowledge of your craft, and what the buying trends are in your product lines.

5) Financial statements that show your income needs, cash flow, budgets, profit and loss statements, break even point, and a financial summary of your business showing all of the above mentioned from the time you began doing business. You might also want to include copies of loan agreements, leases, references, equipment receipts, and business licenses.

An excellent guide to drafting a plan suitable to present to a bank or lender is *Anatomy of a Business Plan* by Linda Pinson and Jerry Jinnett. Included are several sample documents and do-it-yourself forms that every new business owner should know about.

Plans should be easy and give you instant, firsthand information about where your business stands in any given area, at any given moment. Remember that you are:

1) The production craftsperson, the designer and maker of the products you intend to sell. You schedule the time you want to spend working and possibly the hiring of outside help. To attain cost effective means of making your pieces you will need a production schedule of how much, how often and what kind of craft products you will make.

2) The marketing manager, responsible for finding ways to sell your work. You make known to customers why they should buy them you. You evaluate previous sales efforts and plan for upcoming markets with a marketing plan that outlines who will want to buy your products, how

and where you must go to reach these customers, and when or how often to reach them.

3) The financial and planning chief, doing the office work of keeping records, depositing incoming revenue, and paying bills and taxes. You will update bookkeeping records that tell you how much you need to operate your business on a daily, monthly, or yearly basis, and where and when the money will come from.

The following questions will help evaluate your business and update your long term planning:

✓ What is the status of the business in each of the above areas?

✓ Are you pleased with the amount of work you are producing?

✓ Are you satisfied with sales? Are you making enough profit? How is the cash flowing? Is there more going out than coming in?

✓ Have you thought of new products or new ways to sell more of the current inventory?

✓ Have you tried to sell new products to old customers?

Division of labor hours

If you're like many artisans, you work when you feel which is probably much of the time, but not always the same time every day. From recording a normal month's activity, you get a good idea of what you can comfortably produce. You can then estimate the number of shows you can do and stores you can sell to. You can also calculate the exact amount of your labor costs. A production schedule might include the following information:

Figure 10.0 Hours producing

PRODUCTION SCHEDULE				
ITEM	UNITS PER MONTH	SIZE	HOURS PER PIECE	HOURS PER MONTH
Rag rugs	12	36" x 60"	2	24
Dolls	20	18"	3	60
Ornaments	35	3"	1.5	52.5
Sweatshirt	120	Sm/Md/Lg	0.75	90
Earrings	55	1"	1	55

Part 1. How many of each item that you make do you currently produce in a month's time? What is the average number of hours it takes you to make each piece?

Figure 10.1 Hours selling

HOURS SPENT SELLING					
MONTH	CRAFT SHOWS	HOME SHOWS	STORES	MAIL ORDER	TOTAL
Jan.	0	6	4	5	15
Feb.	12	4	3	6	25
March	35	0	0	1	36
April	12	0	1	0	13

Part 2. How many hours do you spend selling? This includes hours involved in doing a crafts show, making

presentations or time talking to prospective customers, and writing or designing promotional material.

Figure 10.2 Hours doing office work

HOURS SPENT FOR OFFICE WORK	
MONTH	TOTAL
Jan.	12
Feb.	15
March	8
April	24

Part 3. How many hours do you spend per month doing office or paper work, including paying bills, ordering supplies, and evaluating your business?

Marketing plan

A marketing plan, simply explained, is a list of items you make, the market groups that will buy these products, and the actions you will take to reach these markets. If you have just started selling, you won't have previous records to use in evaluating your market strategies. That's okay, just guess. It's the writing process that is important. Once you start making written outlines of what actions you will take, you are in a better position to carry out those plans.

Use the information in Chapter 1 to help you choose a line of craft products you think will sell. Define the different kinds of interest groups most likely to purchase these items.

Then write down all of the different possible ways of getting your product in front of these potential buyers. After your first year in business, you should have enough information to evaluate sales and profitability of all your products and markets.

Keep a sales inventory record like that in Figure 10.3 to track how items sell in each market. Transfer sales data from the sales report forms to the inventory records each month. Sales at craft shows are easily tracked when you use a report form like the example of a Craft Show Report shown in Figure 3.2, page 65. This form lists the sales, expenses, and other important information about a craft

Figure 10.3 Inventory of craft items by markets

TOTAL SALES BY MARKETS FOR: August, 1993						
MARKET	dolls	belts	glass figure	wall hanging	handbag	TOTAL
SHOWS	117	56	26	12	5	216
HOME PARTIES	11		13	3	6	33
STORES			12	7	24	43
MAIL ORDER	34		10			44
CATALOGS	2		30	2	19	53
REPS	18		22		14	54
TOTAL	182	56	113	24	68	443

Figure 10.4 Wholesale sales report

WHOLESALE SALES: August, 1993						
ACCOUNT NAME	QT	ITEM	PRICE	TOTAL SALES	LESS COMM.	NET SALES
Brown Gallery	8	scarves	30.OO	240.OO		240.OO
Unique Catalog	24	earring	8.5O	204.OO		204.OO
Betty G./rep	18	pillows	19.OO	342.OO	-51.3O	290.7O
Bill W./rep	23	lamps	37.OO	851.OO	-170.2O	680.8O
					TOTAL	1415.5O

show. You can also use this report for mall shows, renaissance fairs, and home boutiques. Every sale is listed with a description of its contents, color, and amount of the sale. You can find at a glance, all the details you need about how each item in your line is doing.

Sales from stores, galleries, sales reps, and catalogs can be recorded on the Wholesale Sales Reports in Figure 10.4. Again, there are places for content, color, and sale amount. There is also an entry space for commissions so you can total the cost of using reps or agents when selling to wholesale accounts.

A marketing plan really begins to work when you assign priorities to each activity that you plan for selling each of your products. By combining the data from Chapters 1 and 2 and the sales reports, you can learn where to focus time, energy and resources to achieve maximum profits and cut potential losses. The more you know about your sales, the more accurate your calculations will be. You have enough information now to make a priorities worksheet.

In Figure 10.5 on the following page, consider every product's total of sales, market variables, profit, and ease of selling. Each entry is also allowed space for writing in actions. Here you can list the activities needed to increase or decrease a product's production, marketing, or pricing. A marketing worksheet can be for any period of time you choose. But, it will be easier to do your record keeping on a consistent basis like monthly, quarterly, and yearly. In the example, number of units sold, variables, profit, and ease, each receive values according to the examples that follow.

Units sold: Enter the number of pieces of this product sold for the period of time the worksheet covers.

Variables: Assign a value for the variables that further an item's potential sales. For instance: a product that will sell in all four seasons of the year will receive 4 points, one that will sell both wholesale and retail will receive two points, and so on.

Profit: Use the information in Chapter 2 to learn the profit gained from any item. Assign numbers 1 to 10, giving the highest profit items '10'.

Ease of selling: This value is a measure of the ease and enjoyment of the sales process; again using a scale of 1 to 10, with 10 the most pleasing.

When you have assigned number values to each product, add them up. Projects that will make the best use of time, money and energy will generally be those with the highest totals. Whenever you introduce a new product, enter as much of the above information that you have about it. You can now know what to do with each item that you make. You may choose to increase production on pieces that result in higher profits in the markets that are performing best and cut production of work and markets that aren't selling. Write down marketing plans for each product you make. Knowing priorities will help you do tasks most important first.

If you don't organize, you're chances of success become just that — chances, and statistics say not good chances either. Once you know the big picture of products, costs, and markets, the next step is to act. All the planning in the world won't mean anything, if you don't put it into action. And actions work best when they originate from intelligent, focused choices.

Figure 10.5 Marketing priorities worksheet

MARKETING PRIORITIES WORKSHEET				
	PILLOW	RAG RUG	LAMP	WOODEN TOY
MARKET	craft shows	craft shows	catalog	stores
UNITS SOLD	2	17	23	117
VARIABLE INFLUENCES	8	12	8	16
ITEM PROFIT	7	6	3	8
EASE OF SELLING	3	5	9	8
TOTAL POINTS	20	40	43	149
ACTIONS TO TAKE	cut production in half; keep for variety	do more craft shows	lower materials costs, find more catalogs	contact sales reps to increase store accounts

Chapter 11
Using Promotional Material

Throughout your promotional material, maintain a consistency of your image, typestyles, and colors. This means business cards, letterheads, envelopes, brochures, and flyers should use the same styles and color inks to make your name more memorable to the reader.

There are many printers that make business cards, color post cards, brochures, and flyers at varying rates and quantities. You can find local printers listed in the Yellow Pages. Another resource is the *Directory of Book, Catalog and Magazine Printers* by John Kremer which lists over 780 printers nationwide and overseas of catalogs, brochures, books, postcards, and stationery. Printers are indexed by equipment used, printing services, location, toll-free numbers, typesetters, stock recycled papers, design and artwork, 4-color printers, and more. This guide also defines terms used in the printing business and tells you the best ways to work with printers to assure you get exactly what you want.

When you contact a printer, ask them to send samples of their work. Get samples from five or six different companies before you make a choice. Often the same company will produce photo cards, business cards, brochures, flyers, and catalogs. Compare them to know if what they produce is what you want. Shopping around before you order any kind of promo material can result in big savings. I have found inexplicable price differences, sometimes as much as $100 or more for the same printing.

Two companies with quality brochures and postcards at competitive prices are: MWM Dexter, 107 Washington, Aurora, MO 65605, (800) 641-3398 and Mitchell Graphics, 2230 E. Mitchell, Petoskey, MI 49770, (800) 841-6793.

Postcards

Postcards are an inexpensive means of promoting yourself that can take the form of the simple US Postcard, printed on the back with your announcement or a color photo postcard produced by a print shop. A professionally done card can have your company name and address on the back side and a photo of your craftwork on the front. You can also use these as special sale notices or invitational notes by creating a label with show date information to stick on near your address.

If you choose to sell through art and craft shows, you don't need to advertise the event, because show promoters take care of that. A good promoter will have spent several thousand dollars on radio, TV, billboards and newspaper ads to draw in the crowds. What you should do, however, is send out invitational postcards to customers in a city where you are returning to do a show you have exhibited at in the past.

Business cards

For business cards, the expense of having 500 nicely done cards is reasonable. However, for local craft shows, you could easily make a neat hand-done card using card stock paper from a local office supply store, a rubber stamp and a set of ink pens. Make several different cards and save the designs you don't use for future ideas. Shown is a simple card my wife, Dianne, designed with the use of a rubber stamp. This card doubles as a hang tag.

There is small expense in the self-made card and a card with an old-fashioned, hand done look is a sales plus, especially at craft shows.

Figure 11.0 Sample of home made business card

A big advantage of making your own business card is you can change it to target your sales efforts if you see an opportunity for which your current card is inappropriate. For instance, you might want one card for craft show sales and another for store accounts.

If you want to place your work in more than one store in the same area, use another card with a different company name to ensure no conflicts with your other accounts. Many stores don't want your address or phone to appear on the work they buy from you; they fear the loss of sales when customers go to you directly. A solution is to print your address and phone information at the bottom of the card, then cut it off when attaching the cards to pieces for sales to stores.

With increased sales, it becomes more cost-effective to have cards printed. Five hundred business cards will last a year unless you give them out at shows. When you do craft shows, many persons come into your booth and ask for your card. Many of these persons collect cards as their way of leaving without buying anything. Why should you pay for this?

Some craftspersons tell me they never give out cards at craft shows unless it is to a paying customer or a prospective wholesale buyer. In my first two years of doing shows, I gave cards to everyone that asked. I had cards printed twice in quantities of 500, so I must have handed out nearly 1,000 cards. Out of those, no sales came, nor phone calls, nor leads. Now, I only hand out cards to store owners who give me their card in exchange.

As an alternative to saying 'no' to a customer asking for a card, I tell them *"I'm sorry, I'm out, can I put your name on my mailing list and send you information when I will be doing another show here?"* Persons who agree to do this qualify as legitimate prospects for your customer mailing list.

Care labels

You should have a label on every piece that tells the contents, your name as manufacturer, country of origin, and care or cleaning instructions. This is a legal require-ment for textiles, fabric, wool, or clothing. For more exact federal guidelines on labeling and packaging of products, write the Federal Trade Commission, 6th and Pennsylvania Ave. NW, Washington, DC 20580.

Many label making companies have a line of care labels ready to sew in. They also make customized name and care tags from your designs. I ordered sew-in labels to match my business cards and letterheads. This helps build a consistent image easily remembered. Here is a list of label suppliers:

Alpha Impressions, 4161 S. Main St., Los Angeles, CA 90037.

Charm Woven Labels, Box 30027, Portland, OR 97230, (503) 252-5542.

GraphComm Services (for hang tags), P.O. Box 220, Freeland, WA 98249, (800) 488-7436.

Heirloom Woven Labels, Grand Central Post Office, P.O. Box 2188, New York, NY 10163, (212) 620-2767.

Sterling Name Tape Co., Inc., P.O. Box 1056, Winsted, CT 06098, (203) 379-5142.

Hang tags

Every piece should have a hanging tag that gives details about your product, the way it is produced, and you, the artist. Your name should become synonymous with the quality of what you make. Increase the personal message of promotional material by including a story about you, your materials, equipment, where you make your craft, or anything else of interest. Your personal story is an added sales booster that can be incorporated into all promotional material. If you work in a location with historical significance, emphasize this in the story.

Once at a craft show, a man who was admiring my work asked me if I would be interested in placing some of my pieces in his family's gallery. He was an eighth generation weaver of the well known Chimayo weavers north of Santa Fe, New Mexico. What a great sales tool that is, but that's probably more history than many of us can come up with.

Education, grants, awards, and foreign studies add to your credentials, too. Write about the techniques you use and your tools. Almost every aspect of what you do in your craft is interesting to a potential buyer. For additional ideas on hang tags, look at craft items displayed in galleries and stores.

Brochures

For sales to wholesale accounts, a carefully designed brochure is essential. Not only does the brochure remind the store owner or buyer about you, it conveys the impression of professionalism and staying power. This is important in getting sales at larger trade shows. If you make items that will be marketed through direct mail, you will want to include a brochure whenever you do a mailing. A brochure promotes your work without your personal sales presentation.

Collect several catalogs and mail order ads with brochures that have products like yours. Lay them all out and look at them. What attracts you to one or another of these? This is an easy way to get ideas on how you will want yours to look. Graphics designers recommend that at least one third of the page should contain graphics or photos.

In writing headlines, stress the benefits of your products. Emphasize what makes your work different or special. Your words will be more effective if you clearly state how the customer will gain by buying your product. For example: "Feel warm and cozy tonight with a _____ handwoven throw," "Light up your love life with earrings from_____," or "Impress your home buyer with handcrafted furniture from_____."

Create a separate page for the price list and order form. Make it clear to the customer exactly what you want them to do, as "Order today, Send your check to: (your name)," or "Use your MasterCard for easy payment." Creating the order form as a separate page gives you the flexibility of using the same brochure for both retail and wholesale promotions. Be sure to include a blank order form with every order you ship.

If you do a large wholesale business, chances are you will be redoing the brochure regularly and it may be more cost effective to include prices on the brochure page. Your product line will probably change at least once a year. This means new photos and layout work. If you mail to fifty stores or more, you'll want something more than a hand done flyer.

A well produced brochure becomes a statement of the size and image of your business. For a beginner with few accounts, the cost of preparing and printing color brochures is not worth it. In a few hours and for much less expense, you can design and produce much of the necessary materials using a local copy shop to run off as much as you need.

Be sure your sales material contains clear instructions on where and how to place an order. Recently, I was designing a catalog of books. Under pressure to get them distributed by a certain date, I hastily produced the material. On my way to an event to distribute the material, an unexpected delay prevented me from making the deadline. Reconciled to the inevitable, I thought to take another look at the layout. I found that in my haste, I had left out the name and address for customers to order from.

Promotional material can also take the form of packaging. The public buys the packaging of a product because it raises the value they perceive in an item. One successful fiber artist packages every scarf or shawl in an ornate box with full color photography on all sides. Although the artist's work could easily stand on its own merits, selling it in a beautiful box makes it more attractive and the artist can ask a higher price.

Photos of your work

Photos and slides can be used for getting into juried shows, in a brochure, catalog, or log book of your projects, to accompany feature articles about your work, and in a portfolio to make presentations when seeking commissions. Get the best photos of your products that you can afford. You are competing with other artisans as well as commercially made products.

Pictures should show how clothing looks on a customer; how rugs look in a nicely furnished room or office; or how a woman's earrings look dangling from her ears. If one photographer can't give you that look, find another one. A customer sees and remembers the pictures. No money is saved by taking cheap shots. Have photos taken of your best pieces, you at work making your craft, and head shots of you. Make a photo file to use for any media or jurying needs. As mentioned before, you may need several sets of slides to apply for shows with simultaneous application deadlines.

When shooting for jury purposes, use a backdrop that is neutral or flat black. Your craft work should fill the picture as much as possible. Lighting and focus should eliminate shadows and give depth of field to the piece. Halogen lights give the most white of artificial lighting. Fluorescent lighting casts a bluish tint and incandescent casts a reddish tint. A book that deals with the subject of jury slide standards is

Photographing Your Craftwork by Steve Meltzer. The information will be useful if you intend to shoot your work. Another source of photography tips is *Photographing Your Artwork* by Russell Hart. If you decide to photograph your work, a source of discount camera suppliers, equipment, and services is *The Shutterbug*, 5211 S. Washington Ave., Titusville, FL 32780, (407) 268-5010.

Learn about what juries look for so that you can provide guidelines for your photographer to produce the kind of pictures that will help get you accepted into shows. To find an experienced crafts' photographer, check the classifieds in *The Crafts Report.* Request samples of their previous work to compare to your own needs.

Chapter 12
What to Do if Your Work isn't Selling

What do you do if your work isn't selling? Get a job, right? Wrong! At least, not until you have analyzed your situation thoroughly. Before you give up, try some of the methods for increasing a product's sales in this chapter. Begin by asking these questions:

√ Are the markets, I am trying to sell to, receptive to my work? If not, where else will my products be in demand?

√ Am I using the wrong colors, materials, or designs?

√ Can I increase the "perceived value" of my work to make it more attractive?

√ Are my prices too high or too low?

Market receptivity

Often you will find pieces of your work selling well in stores and going nowhere at art and craft shows, and vice versa. Some items simply don't sell in every market, but this doesn't mean the product won't sell elsewhere or that you should stop making it. One fall season, I produced several different garments that I considered my most creative work in six years. I was so confident of the prospects for the new pieces, I signed up for more shows than usual. What a nasty shock I had when the buying public at the fairs overlooked every one of the new designs. I was so discouraged, I was ready to give up weaving completely.

As a last ditch effort, I decided instead to show the work to some prospective store buyers. They loved the designs and took every one of the new pieces. Before this time, my sales in stores had been minimal. Because of the reception of the new work, I approached more stores and opened several good accounts. I felt all along there was nothing wrong with the latest pieces. I simply had been unaware of the possibility that they were not right for the craft show customer. Not surprisingly, the pieces that always sold well at the craft shows impressed the store owners least.

As in the above example, sometimes the craft shows you get into aren't good measures of your work's saleabilty. Read as many different reviews of a fair as you can find. Talk to recent exhibitors. Be discriminating when selecting which shows to do. Read the craft show guides listed in the Appendix for review information. Show performances can change quickly from year to year.

I once signed up for a show at the Astrodome in Houston, put on by a producer out of California. Their first year's promotional efforts had drawn huge crowds, including some of my own family. Since I had a chance to visit folks and a place to stay, I took the risk of doing their second year's show. My sales for the three day weekend exceeded $3,000.

The next year, I had a conflict of schedule and couldn't return, so I told a friend about the show and she was accepted. Her work was similar to mine, yet she only had sales around $2,000. This didn't seem that bad, so the following year, I thought about trying it again myself.

I should have guessed something was wrong when the show sales person called me before I even sent in an application. They said there weren't many spaces left, but because I was a previous exhibitor, I could still get in. I kept putting off the decision until a month before the show, which is usually too late to get in. But the sales person called me one more time to assure me I had a space if I wanted to come. She told me I could even pay at the time of the fair.

By then, I knew something had happened. Either another show in town was scheduled for the same weekend or the promoters just couldn't get enough craftspersons to sign up. I decided to do the show anyway. Sure enough, there were only half as many craft exhibitors as before. Crowds were thin and sales were bad. I barely pulled in $800 for the show and ended with about $400 in expenses. Again, there was nothing wrong with my work, I simply was in the wrong show at the wrong time.

Change your display

If the public is attending but not coming into your booth at craft shows, change your display. It may cost you money to buy better fixtures, but if no one is buying your pieces, you're wasting money to do the show anyway. Check out how other booths look, including other crafts, not just artists in your media.

If you sell clothing, the kind of hangers you use to display clothing will change the appearance of a garment. When I first started doing craft shows, I went for the cheapest hangers I could find. I found some plastic ones priced at six for $1 and thought this was great. By chance, someone going out of the clothing business gave me about twenty hangers with straight shoulders and swivel hooks to hang by. Pieces hanging on the straight hangers looked more as it will on a human shoulder compared to the slanted cheap hangers. Swivel hooks also make it easier to hang items in different display positions. Customers find it easier to look through the racks, too. I found a local used fixture store that sold me more of the straight swivel hangers for about .25 each. I also bought a bundle of inexpensive no-slip foam envelopes to go on each hanger.

Earrings sell better standing up than laying flat. Christmas ornaments will look more attractive on a Christmas tree than sitting under a glass case. You can keep your stock in boxes ready to pull out when a customer makes a selection.

How color affects sales

If there is one determinant that will affect your success in selling your craft products more than any other element, it will be the colors you choose to work with. The public buys color — they are moved by it. Sure, you will always find a market for 'natural' colored work, but without the diversity of a wide and luxurious selection of color combinations, you can't compete with the vast array of products vying for your customer's dollars.

For inspiration of alternative color combinations, look through magazines like *Ornament, Vogue, Metropolitan Home, Better Homes and Gardens,* and *Architectural Digest.* Look at the sky, the earth, the grasses, the birds, the mountains, and don't forget the malls. Yes, that's right, the malls. If you want to see a spectrum of what the public buys, take a leisurely stroll through a mall and just let your eyes take in the colors of clothes, accessories, jewelry, art, furniture, and household items. Keep focused on the tones and combinations of colors you see. If you don't go home with at least two or three ideas, you probably forgot the exercise, because you became distracted and bought something.

Often at craft shows, a customer has entered my booth with a color card book showing the colors they are supposed to wear or a piece of fabric that matches furniture they wish to complement with a throw. These colors usually fit into one of four seasonal descriptions: fall, winter, spring, or summer. Even if you aren't attracted to the idea of color charts, you should be aware of colors associated by season so you can match a person with an appropriate color. For more detailed information about personal color charts, read *Color Me Beautiful* by Carol Jackson.

Watch your customers as they look at your pieces. Make notes of which pieces are picked up more than others. If customers continually ask for certain colors, produce a few to see what happens. If they start to sell, make more. Build an inventory with a wide selection. A variety of selection will make sales increase. Give the customer a choice, they love to shop.

Customers buy arts and crafts as an investment in a 'collectible item'. For their dollars, they also want a piece to suit their personal color preferences, home decor and wardrobe, not what's in vogue today and gone tomorrow. Store sales, on the other hand, typically follow the fashion trends.

A few years ago, I tried an experiment to see how closely the public followed the *in* colors. Colors for the coming season were peach and lavender. In the past, I had good success with these colors used separately, so I thought it worth taking a chance. I created several pieces with about 70% peach tones, 25% shades of lavender, and 5% neutral colors. Only one of the pieces sold at craft shows, so I put the rest in stores. Every one of the pieces sold in the time allotted as the color's seasonal trend.

To find out what's coming in color trends, look through fashion and interiors magazines. Gather mail order catalogs like *L.L. Bean, J. Crew, Miles Kimball* and *Eddie Bauer*. They will give you ideas of color expected in garments and home decor, months ahead of the season. Remember though, you only have a couple of months to produce these colors and market them. By the time you are making goods with the same colors that show up in stores, the trend is on its way out. For the interiors market, colors for rugs and household items do not change as rapidly as those in fashion.

Several companies provide color forecasting services like The Color Box, The Color Association of the U.S., and The Color Marketing Group, but service fees make it impractical for a craftsperson in a small business. A more reasonable resource is *The Crafts Report's* monthly column on coming trends. For subscription information, write *The Crafts Report,* Box 1992, Wilmington, DE 19899. Another source of what's happening in the world of color is *Color Trends,* 8037 9th NW, Seattle, WA 98117. This is a beautiful book for all textile artisans, published annually.

By chance, I once met a man who imported ancient textiles from Peru and South America. He acted as a broker to museums and private collectors for centuries old woven fabrics unearthed at archeological digs; I don't know how he got his hands on them. He showed me a few of the unmounted pieces he had that were dated at 2,000 and 3,000 years old. The woven patterns were impressive, but what struck me even more, was the colors the ancient dyers used. Despite the difference between natural dyes and the commercial dyes of industry, the combinations were much like the rich earth tones and pastels popular today.

Changing the materials to improve sales

Try using alternative materials to add texture, glamour, and distinction to your pieces. For example, add shells, braids, ribbons, reeds, antique buttons, leather strips, paper, fringes, dried flowers, etc.. Create a small sample piece to see how these materials work.

I was having good sales for two years with cotton shawls when, for no apparent reason, the public stopped buying them completely. I was hesitant to stop making a classic item, so I changed the content to mohair. The new shawls sold right away. I also increased the price, without a single complaint. I was convinced of the wisdom of the change when I easily sold the mohair shawls again in a city with a warmer climate 900 miles away.

Designing to sell

Are your craft designs not selling? Consider doing some study of competing artists to learn what they do different. Clothing, jewelry, home items, and gift accessories can all be made in hundreds of different ways. Experiment to find what sells.

Some basic design principles can improve attractiveness. A few of these elements include the fact that a rectangle is more attractive than a square, odd numbers create more interest than even, variety and diversity are more exciting than even spacing. Proportion stripes using the Fibonacci Series; a number system in use since medieval times that contains design elements found frequently in nature. Every number in the series is found by adding the two numbers before. For example 1, 1, 2, 3, 5, 8, 13, 21 and so on. In designing a piece with bands of different colors, stripes of one color could be 3", than another color 1", another 5", another 2", a 3" stripe, and then two different 1" bands.

Increasing the perceived value

Perceived value is the worth the customer places on a given purchase. If a piece isn't selling, you can increase its value in the eyes of the customer by various means. One way is to use more expensive materials and emphasize the exclusiveness of the finished piece. Another way is to make use of hang tags, brochures, and packaging to add value to a piece. It is unfortunately true that the public today often buys the 'packaging' of a product instead of the contents. Though this may insult you as an artist, you might as well make use of the tendency.

Is the price too high, or too low?

You might think an item isn't selling because it's overpriced. There is a tendency among new artisans to mark down their products in an attempt to help the situation. This doesn't necessarily work. Unless you have tried and failed to move a piece for several months at a given price, you make a mistake in lowering the price thinking it will sell better. Typically, the opposite is more often true.

I have often found that a piece sold faster by raising the price, than by lowering it. This is because of the perceived value just mentioned. Sometimes the customer sees 'cheap' on a lower price tag and rejects the work as inferior. However you price your pieces, quality of the work should justify the price you are asking. Any product should be designed and completed with attention to all the details.

An alternative is to supplement an inventory of higher price crafts with smaller quality craft items within a price range of $10 to $20. At shows where sales of high-ticket pieces are slow, you can often pull it out of the slumps with sales of inexpensive smaller items.

Improving your sales tactics

Selling what you make can be as natural as the making of it. People see your work, they desire it, they buy it. Sometimes, though, you need to make a few simple efforts when a customer is hesitant or on the verge of walking away. Techniques presented in this section revolve around generating friendliness between you and your buyer. Customers respect you because you are a craftsperson. They buy handcrafted work because of its novelty as much as utility, so you have a ready market for your products. An easy going approach to sales will give you better results and more personal satisfaction. No one likes insensitive sales-persons who mechanically repeat their 'attack' without regard for the human being they are trying to persuade.

Everyone likes to be recognized, it makes them feel valued. It's the key to getting them to like you. Often, customers buy from you because they feel warmly towards you just as much as the attractiveness of your products. The simplest form of recognition is to greet each customer, even if it is only with a simple *"Hello!"* Find out your customer's name. Address them by their first name as often as you can without being obvious about it.

You can learn to remember your customer's names with this simple trick. Think of the silliest image you can involving the person that makes use of all the syllables in the name. For example, Joe Rockefellar: imagine Joe dressed in diapers, barely contained in a huge cradle, rocking. The more ridiculous the image, the more likely you will remember the name. Listen to customers when they talk. Get interested in them. Sales pitches won't help when you aren't listening to what your customer is saying. There is an immense variety of ways you can talk to people by just staying in the moment. Be friendly. Relax and focus on the person. Giving real attention to customers will warm them up to you and what you are selling.

Opening a conversation with a stranger is tough for many. An easy way to start an exchange is to ask an innocuous question that does not require a 'yes' or 'no' response. Any topic will do, as long as it starts a conversation. Avoid using the same lines over and over again with different persons. Think of things at hand, like complimenting them on their jewelry or handbag, or whatever seems natural.

Once you have broken the ice, you can then lead the direction of talk by asking questions that must be answered with 'yes', as when you see a woman wearing an outfit in purples and greens, *"You wear purples and greens well, don't you?"* When you can get the customer to make 'yes' affirmations one after another, you're closing question *"Can I wrap this up for you?"* has a better chance of getting a 'yes' reply.

Ask for the sale

Sometimes the difference between a customer making a purchase and walking away lies in whether you have asked them for the sale. There are many ways to do this without sounding like a car salesman. Examples include: *"Can I write this up for you?;" "Can I put this one in a bag for you?;" "Will you be putting this on your charge card?;" "How would you like to pay for this?;" "I think you'll be pleased;" "Let me take your order for this today."*

At times during your presentation, you will get better results by telling the person what to do. For instance, I have noticed that when I ask customers if they would like to try on a piece they've been looking at, half the time, they say *"No, then I might want it."* This leaves one in an awkward position. As a solution, try this. When you see someone attracted to a piece, pick it up, take it to them and say *"Here, try this on. See how it looks in the mirror."* They rarely refuse and often end up buying. Once a person tries a piece on, you're more than halfway to making the sale.

Stay focused on your intention

Remember, your intention is to sell your work. A relaxed and free flowing exchange can build a good relationship with the customer, but when you are talking, it often happens that your conversation can ramble. Stay focused by remembering the desired result is that the customer makes a purchase.

The more you talk, the greater your chances of saying the wrong thing. With a person you have just met, you never know what that something will be. Keep it simple and relaxed and you'll have better results.

Stress the benefits of your product

In your sales efforts, remember that the customer buys products based on their needs, not yours. Put emphasis on the benefits of buying your item.

"This wool and mohair jacket is so warm, and feels so cozy."

"These rag rugs are incredibly durable. They'll stand up to everyday use for years."

"These rockers are not only relaxing, they're made from the finest oak available."

Product knowledge

The more you know and are able to say about what goes into your workmanship, the more sales you will make. You increase the 'perceived value' the customer places on your product. It also gains you the customer's confidence. Learn about the different materials used in your craft and their history. Fascinating stories will interest your customers. Did you know that most of the world's mohair comes from Angora goats raised in Texas? Where do dyes come from? What is the history of your craft?

Make it easy for customers to buy

Have all the materials you need to complete a sale nearby whenever you make a presentation to a store buyer or exhibit at a crafts show. You need a receipt book, brochures, business cards, price lists, and bags for packaging the sale. At shows, make the money changing as quick as possible, especially when your booth is crowded. Spending too much time with one customer can cause others to leave in a huff.

Selling from a full display

Whenever you do an exhibition or show, have a full display of items for sale. It is a fact of good merchandising; you'll sell more from a full display than one that has empty places.

Have a variety of colors, don't rely strictly on your own taste. Listen to what your customers tell you about colors and watch your sales reports to see what's selling. A color combination that does well in a crafts show may not do well in store sales. Try new combinations of style and color and keep tracking the results.

Promote yourself

Use the free publicity techniques mentioned earlier in Chapter 6. Find out the name of the newspaper life-style editors in cities where you will be doing shows. Send them an introductory cover letter, copies of previous articles about you, awards and speeches you have given, a press release, and photos of you at work. If articles about you appear, make photocopies of them and mount them in small frames to hang in front of your display. This is the most visible place for posting your awards from past competitions and exhibitions. Buyers invest in you as a recognized artist as much as the work they purchase.

Somewhere in the years of your life, you have acquired a story. You may have won a competition with your craftwork. You might be the eighth generation weaver in your family. Your studio is in an abandoned mill that you renovated.

There are many possibilities. We have all had experiences that someone will relate to. Learning how to connect with people through these stories can increase your sales and management effectiveness. As a technique for selling, relating real experiences works. In a world overflowing with hype and glitz, people are hungry for something real. Successful communication, according to the *Dale Carnegie Course on Public Speaking and Human Relations,* arises from relating to people an experience that actually happened to you instead of using memorized sales lines.

Don't apologize

No one likes a loser. It doesn't pay to excuse yourself for being alive, new in business, or inartistic. Avoid making comments as *"I'm sorry, I know my prices are a little high, but I just started."* Your art is a profession and you are an expert. You put in many hours to make each piece. Your work is worth the price.

Looking energetic

Craft and trade shows require long hours with scant relief. It's tempting to sit and relax at times, but many of your customers aren't concerned with how long you've been standing and talking. They will perceive an element of boredom from you if they come upon you sitting down. Outdoor craft show buyers are more forgiving in this, but wholesale trade buyers are often rushed and have no patience for exhibitors who aren't ready to help them immediately.

Chapter 13
Spin-Off Opportunities

When you're in business for yourself, over time you meet and talk to hundreds of different persons. Often these conversations bring you ideas about ways to expand business. Eventually, you may consider financial opportunities related to your craft, though they might lead away from the studio. You may even find yourself drawn full time in one of these other directions.

There are many different options available for income using the knowledge, experience and personal contacts you have gained from your craft business. This chapter offers some ideas for extra or alternative income. Many of these spin-off businesses require as much or more time as producing and selling handcrafted products. At some point in operating a supplementary business, you may be forced to sacrifice doing your craft or hiring others to help in the running of the business.

Teaching workshops

Teaching isn't limited to the famous; if you can do something, you can teach someone else. If you have no teaching experience, you can begin by reading some instructive books on basic techniques and get a picture of how training a student should progress.

Many colleges and universities have continuing education departments that offer many kinds of craft classes. Talk to the dean of continuing education to find out their teacher eligibility requirements. Teachers pay will be fixed, but guaranteed. Usually, you must apply for these kinds of teaching positions several months in advance, so plan far enough ahead to fit your production schedule.

You might also teach through a local craft supply store. Since the store already has a steady stream of customers, you don't have the advertising costs of trying to generate new students. Also, store owners will probably have an established class fee schedule of their own.

If you don't mind the public coming to your home or workplace, teaching from your studio gives you more freedom in setting up class times and controlling fees. You can advertise through putting up flyers at store bulletin boards, placing announcements in craft guild newsletters, craft magazines, local classified papers and the 'community happenings' section of your newspaper. Sometimes when university and community colleges set up continuing education classes, they are taught in the instructor's studios.

Announcements are free, ads cost money; both get your message out, so why pay? When announcing workshops, include all the information anyone needs to take the class like: what you are teaching, when and where the classes are held, who is the instructor, and the cost.

Include a request for advance registration with a deposit. Offering a slight discount for signing up ahead of time can induce more students to apply.

Charge the same for your workshops as others do for the same length classes, unless you offer expertise in some area of skill that is difficult to obtain. Then you can ask more for your time.

Becoming a crafts supplier

When teaching from home, generate a back-end business by selling supplies, books, and equipment to students coming to your studio. This could easily evolve into a full-time retail supply business.

You may be able to expand the business into a mail order operation through classified ads in crafts magazines. I once began selling yarns to other weavers this way and received good response. As a retailer, you will probably get better discounts from the larger wholesalers that you buy from.

If you have a spouse or a friend to mind the store, it's easier. I have come across many craftspeople who after starting a retail business no longer have any time left for their handicraft.

Opening a retail craft store or gallery

Some craftspersons open retail stores to sell their work direct to the public. They carry a large selection of their own pieces plus complementary craftwork to help fill the shelves and displays. Choosing the right location is the most important element for success in a retail venture. An area of a city that has a thriving tourist industry is an excellent choice.

In a high traffic tourist area, customers are there to buy. You can see this by just hanging out for a day and watching. If you want a stronger criteria for deciding, you can predict a measure of your success by the number of similar businesses operating in the area.

Competition is not bad. In fact, if there is more than one business operating like the one you have in mind, it is a good sign. *The Owner's and Manager's Market Analysis Workbook For Small to Moderate Retail and Service Establishments* by Wayne Lemmon, gives helpful guidelines for estimating your market's possibilities through measuring your competitors.

Taking any location with cheap rent simply to get your business open can be disastrous. Inexpensive rent can't possibly make up for slow sales in a low traffic area.

A friend of mine with no previous business experience, recently married and they decided to open a consignment craft gallery. She had recently left a job with a similar kind of gallery in Maryland and had acquired some knowledge and enthusiasm for this kind of business. They looked at several possible locations; one was a space that had become available in Santa Fe, NM. I was hoping they would take it, because they would be assured of a regular flow of tourist traffic, despite high rent; Santa Fe has many shops and galleries carrying handcrafted work.

Another location, the one they ended up taking, was in a small town, thirty miles away. They chose a building there because the rent was cheap and the storefront was near the downtown area. They also wanted to live in the low stress environment of a small town. When they first introduced me to their idea, their intent was to persuade many different hand-crafters to place work in the store on consignment, which I did because we were friends.

They opened for business in December, weeks later than planned due to unexpected delays and last minute changes. Pre-Christmas shopping was almost finished, but sales came in that would, if continued month to month, have kept them afloat.

Unfortunately, they weren't aware that many retail store sales drop in January and February. Daily sales fell after the first of the year, far below the point of breaking even. Tension mounted between them and my friend had to take a full time job to help pay the store's bills.

Despite this, they managed to sell one of my pieces and sent a check. But when I deposited it, it came back from the bank marked "insufficient funds." After a few weeks and several phone calls, I finally received a money order. Later, I heard the store closed and they divorced because the business difficulties came between them. It was sad to see, but the lesson of their example will not be forgotten.

Not every retail venture is such a failure. A successful store can bring in huge profits over time. Many owners of going stores even open second and third outlets. *The Crafts Report* often includes feature articles about craftspersons who have retail success stories.

One retail survival trait is the owner's ability to provide exclusive merchandise to customers. Department stores trying to offer everything are losing business to shops that cater to specific niches in fashion and special interest.

If you intend to sell other crafts besides your own, you should educate yourself and your salespersons about the different media, how they are made, and the artisan's background. Hangtags with information as that described in Chapter 11 should be attached to every piece.

Before you open a store, list all the possible monthly expenses including getting a business license and fictitious name, signs, rental or lease deposits, first and last month rental payments at commercial rates, insurance against fire, theft and other loss, telephone at business rates, utilities, advertising, employees, inventory, fixtures and office supplies. Don't forget travel and auto expenses. Then, after all of that, add about 10%.

Also, add in how much you will pay yourself, though you may hold off drawing a salary for a few months. If you have a spouse that can help with your other financial obligations, you are in a better position. You should plan to cover the operating expenses from your own pocket for the first year.

If you can't, wait until you either have the money or can secure backing from friends or relatives. Almost all new business failures within the first five years are because of inadequate capital and poor planning.

If you intend to open a gallery of handcrafted work, take a lesson from other stores and get your inventory on consignment. It costs you nothing except the bookkeeping and many craftspeople prefer to get their work in the stores rather than have it sitting at home in a box.

A cautionary word about taking in craftwork on consignment; in a few cases, a craftsperson doing both show and store business will use their better inventory in the shows and 'dump the dogs' with consignment shops hoping the stores will do the work of selling them. Jury the crafts you want to carry to maintain a level of quality.

Make the shop more appealing by demonstrating your craft and inviting other artists to demonstrate as well. The public likes to learn what goes into the process. This allows them to see the amount of work in a piece and raises their perceived value of handcrafted products.

Consider all the details involved, especially choosing a location and having the capital to pay expenses until the business can support itself. For trends and tips in retail store operations, see periodicals like *Giftware News, Profitable Crafts Merchandising,* and *Accessory Merchandising.*

Starting a crafts cooperative

See page 16, in Chapter 1 for a description of cooperatives for craftspersons. As a new start-up business, joining with others to form a cooperative costs less than opening your own store. The federal government can even offer you assistance in starting a co-op venture. *The Cooperative Approach to Crafts* by Jan Halkett, William Seymour, and Gerald Ely is available FREE from: U.S. Dept. of Agriculture, Agricultural Cooperative Service, Washington, DC 20250. Another resource is *We Own It: Starting & Managing Cooperatives and Employee Owned Ventures* by Bernard Kamoroff, Bell Springs Publishing, Box 640, Laytonville, CA 95454.

A newsletter specifically for artisan's cooperatives is *The Artisan's Commonwealth,* published by Stephen Clerico, Box 192, Free Union, VA 22940, (804) 978-4109.

Producing craft shows

If you have done home parties with a couple of other craftspersons, you have the basic working knowledge needed to produce a craft show. It's easy to start with small, manageable events and then expand your operation to include more vendors, renting a larger space, and doing more publicity to bring in bigger crowds. There are many important details involved in producing a successful craft event. City permits are required. Advertising and publicity must be arranged well in advance. Craft exhibitors need to know far enough ahead of time to plan for the show. Also, there are countless other considerations like insurance, emergency procedures, and extra help with organizing the event.

Payoffs from producing a well-run craft shows can be good. Even a small, weekend event with 50 participants each paying $50 for a space will gross you $2,500. You may also want to set up your own booth in a prime location of the show. Two resources that give more detailed information on becoming a show promoter are: *How to Put On a Great Craft Show; First Time and Every Time* by Dianne and Lee Spiegel, from FairCraft Publishing, Box 5508, Mill Valley, CA 94942, (415) 924-3259, and *The Arts Festival Work Kit* by Pam Korza and Dian Magie, from Arts Extension Services, Div. of Continuing Education, University of Massachusetts, Amherst, MA 01003, (413) 545-2360.

Writing

Anyone can write about what they know. If you have ever experienced writer's block, writing about something is the quickest solution to unravel your potential creativity. Look through *Books In Print* in the library under the subject heading of your craft. The number of books about a given subject suggests the amount of interest the public has toward it and the potential market for sales. If you're proficient in a specific technique or school of design, consider writing how-to articles for the appropriate craft magazines. Payment may be nominal, but as you become known as an expert, you will be sought out as a teacher and lecturer; for a fee, of course.

Becoming a sales rep

Many artisans prefer to work at home and let someone else do the selling. For the person with a love of people, this provides an opportunity to represent several craftspersons' work, travel to different areas and meet with new store owners. To build your business, attend craft shows and introduce yourself to exhibitors. Provide references and your fee and payment schedules. Run classified ads in the craft periodicals like *The Crafts Report*. Also, send your name and information to *The Rep Registry, P.O. Box 2306, Capistrano Beach, CA 92624, (714) 240-3333* and to *Directory of Wholesale Reps for Crafts Professionals*, Northwoods Trading Co., 13451 Essex Court, Eden Prairie, MN 55347, (612) 937-5275. Listings here will bring responses from craft makers.

Earn additional income through referral marketing

Sometimes you find that no matter what you do, you can't seem to earn enough cash to get those things you want. I found I could make extra money through becoming a part-time distributor for a major network marketing company. You can earn anywhere from an extra $300 to $500 per month and it doesn't interfere with your current job or business. If you are interested in earning more money while helping others make extra income and can spend 5 to 10 hours per week, write me for more details: James Dillehay, Box 75, Torreon, NM 87061.

Chapter 14
More Success Tips

Here are a few more helpful pointers, all of them having proved useful. Many will save you time and hassles, not to mention, increase your profits.

- <u>Networking</u> with a group who shares your interests opens doors to new opportunities. Many associations exist to help increase contacts, expand marketing efforts, provide information about funding, insurance, and legal advice. By joining or contacting one or more of these organizations, you can stay informed through newsletters and journals of timely events like legal issues, competitions, conventions, and exhibitions. You also get the advantage of learning about other artists, designers, and purchasers of art and craft work. Look for a local craft guild near you. These groups often do cooperative selling ventures for their members.

- <u>Organize yourself:</u> Get your ideas down on paper. Make frequent notes. Create files for ideas, receipts, customer addresses, and supplier information.

- <u>Stay informed about business:</u> Publications for home businesses can help you gain insights into your crafts business. Magazines and newsletters are a great source for production tips, supplier information, and fresh new ideas. See the Appendix for listings of *The Crafts Report* and *Barbara Brabec's Self-Employment Survival Letter.*

- <u>Take classes:</u> The more you know, the more you can do. Increase your technical skills and gain competitive advantages in the marketplace. Craft shops and schools usually offer courses in craft and art techniques. This is a good way to pick up tips for faster production methods.

- <u>Work from home:</u> Start making products at home. Since you are already paying utilities, rent, or house payments, you won't increase your expenses and you can still spend time with your family.

- <u>Use what you got:</u> Before spending money for equipment and supplies, honestly assess whether you need them. Be creative with materials that have gone unused for awhile. Once, I took some ghastly colored yarns, indisputably useless, and over-dyed them with great results.

- <u>Cut costs by sharing expenses:</u> I share studio space with three other craftspersons, saving on rent and utilities. As a group, we also help generate enthusiasm for each other's work and business. We sometimes make large materials orders together to receive bigger discounts. Sometimes we share booth space at craft shows.

- <u>Prepare for 'hot sales' times:</u> Be ready for the good selling seasons, like the months before Christmas, with plenty of inventory. Once the season is past, it's several months before sales pick up. Use a production quota to insure you have the goods. Order your materials far enough ahead of the production time so that you aren't ruined by out-of-stock problems with suppliers. Budget so that you'll have the money to buy what is needed.

- <u>Get phone service in your own name</u>: The phone company will charge you a higher rate for a business phone than for service in your name.

- <u>Save on travel expenses</u>: Lower your travel costs by doing shows in cities where you have friends and relatives. If you do many shows, chances are you will make good friends with other craftspeople. When your show schedules coincide, why not share motel costs?

- <u>Do your own building and maintenance</u>: Cut down auto expenses. Learn how to do easy repairs on your car like changing your oil and tune-ups. Build, or find a friend to help you construct your display booths, inventory shelves or tables for your studio.

- <u>Make mistakes pay</u>: If your project doesn't turn out for some reason, write it down and think of other ways to use what you've made. Can a piece be taken apart and rebuilt?

- <u>Get payments for orders in advance</u>: Whenever a customer wants something special made, ask for payment in advance. When a new store account places an order, require them to prepay or accept the shipment C.O.D.

- <u>Look at examples of successful craft businesses</u>: *The Crafts Report* is full of success stories by craftspersons like you. Their stories give helpful tips and inspiration.

- <u>Contract the drudgery</u>: If detail and finishing work drive

you crazy, hire someone to do it for you. You can pay
them by the hour or by the piece; this gives you more
time to design and sell.

● Think BIG: Save time and increase profits by "ganging
up" your production. For example, work from several
piles of assembled raw materials. This cuts down
production time per piece, increasing profits.

● Avoid undercutting your store accounts: If you do a craft
show in the same town where you have a store account,
be sure to charge the same retail price that they are
asking for similar products.

● Use contracts in all business arrangements: When working
with galleries, designers, or large exhibitions, draw up
agreements clearly defining liability, how pieces will be
shipped, who pays for the shipping, and who's liable if
something goes wrong. Require purchase orders from
stores. Clarifying these things in advance can save you
hundreds, perhaps thousands of dollars in the event of
confusion or unexpected misfortune.

● Free and low cost help: Free advice can be obtained in
many forms. Libraries provide books and references on
every subject. Large organizations have toll free numbers
and will send you free information. For instance: Visual
Artists Information Hotline, (800) 232-2789; Small
Business Administration national information, (800) 827-
5722; For information on getting low cost accounting
advice, write to the Accountants for the Public Interest,
1012 14th St. NW, Suite 906, Washington, DC 20005.

● Keep your eyes open for new opportunities: If you come
across a store that sells handcrafted items, but not your
craft, approach them about carrying your work. Adding

a new product line will increase sales for both of you.

- <u>Use suppliers that offer credit terms of 30 days to pay for purchases:</u> Many suppliers will extend you a month if you can come up with a couple of references. Approach the major suppliers as a retail supplier if you want to receive wholesale discounts. If you set up a retail business to other craftspersons, you can buy supplies for about 50% of the average retail price. If you teach classes, resell these supplies to students at the full price.

- <u>Hire the physically disadvantaged:</u> The government has a grant program for businesses that offer training that leads to employment for individuals with handicaps. Contact: Office of Program Operations, Rehabilitation Services Administration, Dept. of Education, Washington, DC 20202.

- <u>Join the American Professional Crafters Guild</u> to get wholesale buying discounts, health/life/property insurance for crafters, credit card processing, professional training and education, book discounts, a bimonthly newsletter devoted to issues like marketing and merchandising strategies, trends, legal and financial issues and more, and other benefits. Annual dues are $45. For more information call 1-630-377-8000 ext. 357 or write: American Professional Crafters Guild, 707 Kautz Rd, St. Charles, IL 60174.

- <u>Save money on your long distance phone bill.</u> Through a network cooperative plan, I've cut my long distance phone costs by 30% and more. Interstate rates anytime of the day are only 12.9 cents per minute in six second increments. Rates within each state vary, but give a tremendous savings over all local carriers. This program is a must for cutting phone costs. For an information brochure, call: W.Snow Discount Long Distance, (505)384-1102.

●   Get proven, cost-cutting tips for your small business. *CostCutters News* is a bimonthly newsletter loaded with ways to reduce all your business expenses. Learn how to reduce travel, insurance, advertising, office supplies, telephone, and many more expenses. One issue alone will give you enough ideas to save many times the cost of a subscription, only $19.95 a year. For a sample issue, send $3.50 to: *CostCutters News for Business*, Box 75, Torreon, NM 87061.

In closing, I would like to wish you the very best in your art or craft business. Remember to be patient and persistent and you will become successful at any venture. Also remember to enjoy what you do, otherwise you might as well be working for someone else.

                                                     J.D.

Appendix A
Organizations

Accountants for Public Interest
1012 14th St. NW Suite 906
Washington, DC 20005
(202) 347 1668

American Artists & Craftsmen
Guild
PO Box 193
Westmont, IL 60559

American Council for the Arts
1 E. 53rd St.
New York, NY 10022
(800) 321-4510

American Craft Association
21 S. Eltings Corner Rd.
Highland, NY 12528
(800) 724-0859

American Society of Artists
P.O. Box 1326
Palatine, IL 60078
(312) 751-2500

American Society of Interior
Designers
608 Massachusetts Ave. NE
Washington, DC 20002-6006

The Artists Foundation
8 Park Plaza
Boston, MA 02116
(617) 227-2787

Arts & Crafts Materials Institute
100 Boylston St.
Boston, MA 02116

Association for Enterprise
Opportunity
500 N Michigan Ave., Ste. 1400
Chicago, IL 60611
(312) 357-0177

Craft Emergency Relief Fund
(CERF)
245 Main St.
Northampton, MA 01060

The Crafts Center
1001 Connecticut Ave., NW
Washington, D.C. 20036
(202) 728 9603

The Foundation Center
79 Fifth Ave.
NY, NY 10003
(800) 424-9836

Graphic Artists Guild
Foundation
11 W. 20th St., 8th Flr.
New York, NY 10011
(212) 463-7730

Handweavers Guild of America
2402 University Ave, Ste. 702
St. Paul, MN 55114
(612) 646-0806

Hobby Industries of America
200 5th Avenue
New York, NY 10010
(201) 794-1133

International Licensing Industry
Merchandisers Ass'n.
350 Fifth Avenue, Suite 6210
New York, NY 10118
(212) 244-1944

International Tapestry Network
PO Box 203228
Anchorage, AK 99520

The Museum Store Association
501 S Cherry St. #460
Denver, CO 80222
(303) 329-6968

National Assembly of
State Arts Agencies
1010 Vermont Ave. NW, Ste 920
Washington, DC 20005
(202) 347-6352

National Association for the
Cottage Industry
PO Box 14850
Chicago, IL 60614
(312) 472-8116

Nat'l Association for the Self-
Employed
Box 612067
Dallas, TX 75261
(800) 232-6273

National Association of Women
Business Owners
1377 K St. NW, Ste.637
Washington, DC 20005

National Endowment for the Arts
1100 Pennsylvania Ave., NW
Room 710
Washington, DC 20506
(202) 682-5448

The National Needlework Ass'n.
650 Danbury Road
Ridgefield, CT 06877

National Tabletop Association
355 Lexington Ave.
NY, NY 10017

Ontario Crafts Council
35 McCaul St.
Toronto, Ontario M5T 1V7
Canada (416) 977-3551

Small Business Administration
Call (800) 827-5722 to locate
your nearest SBA office and
SCORE (Service Core of
Retired Executives)

Society of Arts and Crafts
175 Newbury St.
Boston, MA 02116
(617) 266-1810

Society for Craft Designers
6175 Barfield Rd., #220
Atlanta, GA 30328
(404) 252-2454

Surface Design Association
PO Box 20799
Oakland, CA 94620

Volunteer Lawyers for the Arts
1 East 53rd Street, 6th Floor
New York, NY 10022
(212) 319-2787

Appendix B
Buyer's Directories

Directory of Arts & Crafts Sources ($14.95)
Warm Snow Publishers
P.O. Box 75
Torreon, NM 87061
2,000+ listings of craft buyers, suppliers, organizations, shows

Department Stores
Lebhar-Friedman Inc
425 Park Avenue
New York, NY 10022-3559
Phone: 212-756-5000
No. buyers listed: 900 chains & 950 mail order

Directory of Southern California Buyers, Retailers & Sales Cos.
6318 Vesper Avenue
Van Nuys, CA 91411-2378
Phone: 818-785-8039

Drug Store and HBA Chains
Lebhar-Friedman Inc
425 Park Avenue
New York, NY 10022-3559
Phone: 212-756-5000
No. buyers listed: 2000+ drug store chains

Food Service Distributors
Lebhar-Friedman Inc
425 Park Avenue
New York, NY 10022-3559
Phone: 212-756-5000
No. buyers listed: 3500+ food distributors

Funparks Directory
Amusement Business
PO Box 24970
Nashville, TN 37202
Phone: 615-321-4250
No. buyers listed: 2500 zoos/ other tourist attractions

Gift Shop Directory
Resourceful Research
FDR Station P O Box 642
New York, NY 10022-0642
No. buyers listed: 900 gift shops

Gift, Housewares & Home Textiles
The Salesman's Guide
Reed Reference Publishing
121 Chanlon Road, P O Box 31
New Providence, NJ 07974
Phone: 800-223-1797
No. buyers listed: 12,800 retail stores/$125.00

Health Marketing Buyers Guide
CPS Communications
7200 W Camino Road #215
Boca Raton, FL 33433
Phone: 305-368-9301

Home Furnishings Retailers
Lebhar-Friedman Inc
425 Park Avenue
New York, NY 10022-3559
Phone: 212-756-5000
No. buyers listed: 5100+ distributors

Military Market Buyers' Guide
ARMY Times Publishing Co.
6883 Commercial Drive
Springfield, VA 22159
Phone: 703-750-9000
Military store distributors

Nationwide Men's Wear Buyers
Reed Reference Publishing
121 Chanlon Road, PO Box 31
New Providence, NJ 07974
Phone: 908-665-2818
No. buyers listed: 5700 outlets
men and boy's wear stores/$112

Nationwide Women's Wear
Buyers
Reed Reference Publishing
121 Chanlon Road, PO Box 31
New Providence, NJ 07974
Phone: 908-665-2818
No. buyers listed: 21,500 buyer
women & children's stores/$112

Sheldon's Retail
Phelon, Sheldon & Marsar
15 Industrial Avenue
Fairview, NJ 07022
Phone: 800-234-8804
No. buyers listed: 3200
department and women's stores

Sloan's Green Guide to
Antiques
Dealers - New England
The Antique Press
105 Charles Street #140
Boston, MA 02114
Phone: 617-723-3001

Wholesale Reps for Craft Profs
Northwoods Trading Company
13451 Essex Court
Eden Prairie, MN 55347
Phone: 612-937-5275
No. buyers listed: Wholesaler
reps/$14.95

Women's & Children's Wear
Lebhar-Friedman Inc
425 Park Avenue
New York, NY 10022-3559
Phone: 212-756-5000
No. buyers listed: 5200+ chains

Craft Shop & Gallery Directory
Front Room Publishers
P O Box 1541
Clifton, NJ 07015-1541
Phone: 201-773-4215
No. buyers listed: 1050 craft
stores, catalogs, buyers

Herbal Green Pages
The Herbal Connection
3343 Nolt Road
Lancaster, PA 17601-1507
Phone: 717-898-3017
No. buyers listed: 2000
wholesale/retail listings

Jewelry Buyers
Reed Reference Publishing
121 Chanlon Road, P O Box 31
New Providence, NJ 07974
Phone: 908-665-2818
No. buyers listed: 8,500 buyers
jewelers and gem retailers/$197

Directory of Organic
Wholesalers
California Action Network
Phone: 800-852-3832

Appendix C
Craft Fair Guides

A Step Ahead
2950 Pangborn Rd.
Decatur, GA 30033

Art and Craft News
P.O. Box 26624
Jacksonville, FL 32226
904-757-3913

The ArtFair SourceBook
1234 S. Dixie Hwy, #11
Coral Gables, FL 33146
800-358-2045

Arts & Crafts Catalyst
PO Box 433
S. Whitley, IN 46787

Arts & Crafts Show Guide
P.O. Box 104628
Jefferson City, MO 65110
314-636-0491

Craft Digest
PO Box 155
New Britain, CT 06050

Craftmaster News
P.O. Box 39429
Downey, CA 90239
310-869-5882

The Crafts Fair Guide
Box 5508
Mill Valley, CA 94942
415-924-3259

The Crafts Report
PO Box 1992
Wilmington, DE 19899
800-777-7098

Craft Show Bulletin
Box 1914
Westfield, MA 01086

Early American Life
P.O. Box 8200
Harrisburg, PA 17105

Fairs & Festivals
Arts Extension Service
Div. of Continuing Education
Box 33260
University of Massachusetts
Amherst, MA 01003

Harris Rhodes List
Box 142
La Veta, CO 81055
719-742-3146

Renaissance Shopper Magazine
P.O. Box 422
Riverside, CA, 92502

Southern Arts and Crafts (SAC)
PO Box 159
Bogalusa, LA 70429
800-825-3722

Sunshine Artists Audit Book
1736 N. Highway 427
Longwood, FL 32750
407-332-4944

Appendix D
Wholesale Trade Show Organizers

AMC Trade Shows
1933 S. Broadway, Ste. 111
Los Angeles, CA 90007
(213) 747-3488

American Craft Enterprises
21 S. Eltings Corner Rd.
Highland, NY 12528
(800) 836-3470

American Craft Marketing
Box 480
Slate Hill, NY 10973
(914) 355-2400

Americana Sampler
Box 160009
Nashville, TN 37216
(615) 227-2080

AMC Trade Shows
2140 Peachtree NW, Ste. 2200
Atlanta, GA 30303
(800) 285-6278

Beckman's Gift Show
Industry Productions of America
PO Box 27337
Los Angeles, CA 90027
(213) 962 5424

Contemporary Crafts Market
Roy Helms & Associates
1142 Auahi St., Ste 2820
Honolulu, HI 96814
(808) 422-7362

Chicago Gift, Accessories Mart
222 Merchandise Mart, Ste. 470
Chicago, IL 60654
(800) 677-MART

Creative Fairs Ltd.
New York Renaissance Fest
134 Fifth Ave.
New York, NY 10011

Dallas Market Center
2100 Stemmons Freeway
Dallas, TX 75207
(214) 744 3131

Denver Merchandise Mart
451 E. 58th Ave.
Denver, CO 80216
(800) 289-6278

Fashion Accessory Expo
200 Connecticut Ave.
Norwalk, CT 06856
(203) 852-0500

Festival Productions
2323 Poplar St.
Oakland, CA 94607
(415) 268-8463

George Little Management Co.
10 Bank St., Ste. 1200
White Plains, NY 10606
(914) 421-3200

The Heritage Market
Box 389
Carlisle, PA 17013
(717) 249 9404

Int'l. Fashion Boutique Show
100 Well Ave.
Newton, MA 02159
(617) 964-5100

Karel Exposition Management
Box 19-1217
Miami Beach, FL 33119
(305) 534-7469

Kentucky Craft Market
39 Fountain Place
Frankfort, KY 40601
(502) 564-8076

Market Square Shows
Valley Forge Furniture Market
PO Box 250
Carlisle, PA 17013

Messe Frankfurt International
GmbH, Ludwig-Erhard Anlage 1,
6000 Frankfurt 1, Germany

The Museum Store Association
501 S Cherry St. #460
Denver, CO 80222
(303) 329-6968
(sponsors annual convention/
publishes a quarterly magazine
called the *Museum Store)*

The National Needlework Ass'n.
650 Danbury Road
Ridgefield, CT 06877

NEOCON
222 Merchandise Mart, Ste. 470
Chicago, IL 60654
(800) 677-MART

Oasis Gift Trade Show
1130 E Missouri, Ste. 750
Phoenix, AZ 85014
(800) 344-1237
(602) 230-2717

Northern New England Products
Trade Show / Small Business
Development Center
96 Falmouth St.
Portland, ME 04103
(800) 638-6787

Offinger Management
Box 2188
Zanesville, OH 43702
(614) 452-4541

The Rosen Group
3000 Chestnut Ave., Suite 300
Baltimore, MD 21211
(410) 889 2933

South Eastern Exhibitions
805 Parkway
Gatlinburg, TN 37738

Tradeshow & Exhibit Manager
1150 Yale St., Suite 12
Santa Monica, CA 90403

Western Exhibitors
2181 Greenwich St.
San Francisco, CA 94121
(415) 346 6666

Appendix E
Booth Cover & Display Suppliers

Canopies by Fred
9229 Sand Point Way NE
Seattle, WA 98115

Clark Manufacturing
339 E. Blaine St.
Corona, CA 91718-1303

Creative Energies
1609 N Magnolia Ave.
Ocala, FL 34475

Dealers Supply
P.O. Box 717
Matawan, NJ 07747

DisplayBright
108 Echo St.
Santa Cruz, CA 95060
(800) 995-1723

EZ Up Canopies
3420 N. Dodge Blvd.
Tucson, AZ 85716
(800) 432-7987

Elaine Martin
Box 261
Highwood, IL 60040

Flourish Company
5763 Wheeler Rd.
Fayetteville, AR 72703

Grid Lock Display
P.O. Box 772
Amityville, NY 11701

KD Kanopy
5758 Lamar St.
Arvada, CO 80002
(800)432-4435

John Mee Canopies
Box 11220
Birmingham, AL 35202
(205) 967-1885

Made in the Shade
RT. 1, Box 180
Stockholm, WI 54769
(800) 532-7987

New Venture Products
7441 114th Avenue N., Ste. 606
Largo, FL 34643
(813)545-4899

Quick & Easy, Mike Hutslar
1975 Holly Drive
Concord, CA 94520

Skycap Canopy Company
37 W. 19th St.
New York, NY 10011
(800) 243-9227

Super Awning, Hazel Yoder
5 Town & Country Village, # 545
San Jose, CA 95128

The Supply Source
8805 N. Main St.
Dayton, OH 45415

Appendix F
Magazines & Newsletters

American Artist
1515 Broadway
NY, NY 10036

American Craft Magazine
40 West 53rd St.
New York, NY 10019

American Woodworker
33 E Minor Street
Emmaus, PA 18098-0001

Architectural Digest
5900 Wilshire Blvd.
Los Angeles, CA 90036

Art Material Trade News
6255 Barfield Road
Atlanta, GA 30328-4369

Arts & Crafts Newsletter
50 West Oak Hill Road
Williston, VT 05495-9663

The Artisan's Commonwealth
(newsletter about cooperatives)
Box 192
Free Union, VA 22940

Better Homes & Gardens
1716 Locust Street
Des Moines, IA 50309-3023

Bridal Crafts
701 Lee Street #1000
Des Plaines, IL 60016

Ceramic Arts & Crafts
30595 West 8 Mile Road
Livonia, MI 48152-1798

Ceramic Hobbyist
2175 Sheppard Avenue E. #110
Willowdale, Ontario M2J 1W8
Canada

Ceramics Monthly
1609 Northwest Boulevard
Columbus, OH 43212-2544

Country Business
707 Kautz Road
St Charles, IL 60174

Country Journal
PO Box 8200
Harrisburg, PA 17105-8200

Craft Marketing News
PO Box 1541
Clifton, NJ 07015-1541

Craft News/Ontario Crafts Council
346 Dundas St. W
Toronto, Ontario M5T 1G5
Canada

Craft Supply Magazine
225 Gordons Corner Rd
Manalapan, NJ 07726

Craft Trends/Sew Business
6201 W Howard Street
Niles, IL 60714

Crafts 'N Things
701 Lee Street #1000
Des Plaines, IL 60016

Crafts Magazine
PO Box 1790
Peoria, IL 61656-1790

The Crafts Report
PO Box 1992
Wilmington, DE 19899

*Directory of Arts & Crafts
Sources* ($14.95)
Warm Snow Publishers
P.O. Box 75
Torreon, NM 87061

Early American Life
P.O. Box 8200
Harrisburg, PA 17105

Family Circle
110 Fifth Avenue
New York, NY 10011-5603

Fiber Arts
50 College St.
Asheville, NC 28801

Furniture Today
200 S. Main St.
High Point, NC 27261

Gifts & Decorative Accessories
51 Madison Ave.
NY, NY 10010

Gift & Stationery Business
1515 Broadway, 32nd Floor
NY, NY 10036

Good Housekeeping Magazine
959 Eighth Avenue
New York, NY 10019-3737

Handwoven
201 E. Fourth St.
Loveland, CO 80537

Interior Design Magazine
249 West 17th Street
New York, NY 10011-5300

Ladies' Home Journal
100 Park Avenue 3rd Floor
New York, NY 10017-5516

Lapidary Journal
60 Chestnut Avenue #201
Devon, PA 19333-1312

Leather Craftsman
PO Box 1386
Fort Worth, TX 76101

McCall's
110 Fifth Avenue
New York, NY 10011

Metropolitan Home
750 Third Avenue, 11th Flr.
New York, NY 10017

Metalsmith
5009 Londonderry Dr.
Tampa, FL 33647

Museum Store Magazine
501 S Cherry St. #460
Denver, CO 80222

Nat'l Arts Placement Newsletter
1916 Association Dr.
Reston, VA 22091

Barbara Brabec's Self-
Employment Survival Letter
Box 2137
Naperville, IL 60567

The Network: Marketing Guide
for Artists
P.O. Box 1248
Palatine, IL 60078

Ontario Craft News
35 McCaul St.
Toronto, Ontario M5T 1V7
Canada (416) 977-3551

Ornament
PO Box 2349
San Marcos, CA 92079

Picture Framing Magazine
P.O. Box 420
Manalapan, NJ O7726

Popular Ceramics
PO Box 337
Iola, WI 54945

Popular Woodworking
1041 Shary Circle
Concord, CA 94518

The Professional Quilter
P.O. Box 1628
Wheat Ridge, CO 80034

Profitable Crafts Merchandising
P.O. Box 1790
Peoria, IL 61656

Quilt World
306 East Parr Road
Berne, IN 46711

Redbook
224 West 57th Street
New York, NY 10019-3299

Renaissance Shopper Magazine
P.O. Box 422
Riverside, CA, 92502

Sampler & Antique Needlework
405 Riverhills Business Park
Birmingham, AL 35253-6091

Sew News
PO Box 1790
Peoria, IL 61656

Shuttle Spindle & Dyepot
2402 University Ave, Ste. 702
St. Paul, MN 55114

Surface Design Journal
PO Box 20799
Oakland, CA 94620

Teaching for Learning
(newsletter for fiber arts
teachers)
511 Hahaione St., #18
Honolulu, HI 96825

Threads
63 S. Main St.
Newtown, CT 06470

Today's Woodworker
PO Box 44
Rogers, MN 55374

Tole World
1041 Shary Circle
Concord, CA 94518

Weaver's
PO Box 1525
Sioux Falls, SD 57101-1525

Woodsmith
2200 Grand Avenue
Des Moines, IA 50312-5306

Wearable Wonders
306 East Parr Road
Berne, IN 46711

Woodworker
380 Lexington Avenue
New York, NY 10168-0001

Weekend Woodcrafts
1041 Shary Circle
Concord, CA 94518

Woodworker's Journal
PO Box 1629
New Milford, CT 06776-1629

WestArt
Box 6868
Auburn, CA 95604

Workbasket
700 West 47th Street #310
Kansas City, MO 64112

Wildfowl Carving & Collecting
PO Box 1831
Harrisburg, PA 17105-1831

Recommended Reading

All of the books on the following pages are available by mail order and come with a no-risk, money back guarantee. To order, see page 216.

The Basic Guide to Pricing Your Craftwork
by James Dillehay

One of the most often asked questions from craftpersons selling their work is *"How much should I charge?"* Whether you are a seasoned professional or just starting, this guide will give you the tools to beome more profitable and competitive. You will learn basic formulas for pricing your craftwork in selling retail or wholesale, how to use pricing strategies to increase sales, how to increase the perceived value of your products, how to know if you are really making a profit, how to keep records, and how to manage your time and workspace to reduce your labor costs and boost productivity. You also get examples of many tax advantages from your craft business. Your success as a professional crafter may very well depend on what you find in this guide. 160 pages, illustrated, charts, index.
Item #400 $12.95

"An excellent resource . . . a well organized book is nothing without solid information and the book delivers here."
The Crafts Report

Craft Business Forms Kit

Over 25 master forms for your craft business. Set of 8.5" by 11" pages you can copy or adapt for your own use. Includes recordkeeping forms like: Cash Flow Statement, Depreciation, Telephone Log, Mileage Log, Time Log, Weekly Inome, Weekly Expense, Travel & Entertainment and many more.
Item #101 $9.95

Small Time Operator, *How to Start Your Own Business, Keep Your Books, Pay Taxes & Stay Out of Trouble!*
by Bernard Kamoroff, C.P.A.

A complete guide for anyone starting a small business. Covers everything including permits and licenses, insurance, financing, leases, business plans, bookkeeping, taxes, employees, partnerships, corporations, trademarks, dealing with the IRS, and much more. Recommended by the U.S. Small Business Administration and the National Society of Public Accountants. 216 pages, softcover, illustrated.
Item #106 $16.95

We Own It: *Starting & Managing Co-ops, Collectives & Employee Owned Ventures*
by Peter Honigsberg, attorney & Bernard Kamoroff, C.P.A.

A clearly written guidebook with complete legal, tax and management information to start and successfully operate all types of cooperatives. Covers nonprofit, for-profit and cooperative corporations, employee stock ownership plans and all other forms of employee owned businesses. Recommended by the National Consumer Co-op Bank, Co-op America, and many regional co-op organizations. 165 pages, softcover, illustrated.
Item #108 $14.00

Directory of Craft Shops & Galleries *by Adele Patti*

Describes 1,052 craft marketing opportunities for crafts people seeking buyers and other outlets for their handcrafted items. Listed by state with complete information on the specific crafts

buyers want. Includes their retail price range, purchase/consignment info, year established, number of artisans presently represented, and whether hang tags are accepted. Also includes mail-order craft catalogs, directories, sales reps, craft home party organizers, and craft cooperatives.
Item #127 $12.95

Directory of Craft Malls & Rent-A-Space Shops

by Adele Patti. Describes 136 craft malls and rent-a-space shops nationwide. Listed by state with complete information on the specific hand crafts wanted. The Directory also includes their retail price range, best selling price, rental/lease information, year established, type of spaces available, when sales are paid, number of artisans presently represented, and more.
Item #126 $12.95

Selling in Craft Malls *by Patricia Krauss.*

This well thought out guide helps you define a craft mall, shows you how craft malls operate, tells you the pros and cons, helps you locate stores, gives you tips on evaluating stores and displays, and instructs you on marketing and inventory management. Krauss capsulizes the most frequently asked questions by beginners in the field. She helps the reader know what to ask and what to expect of a mall operator. *"This is what makes this one of the most invaluable guidebooks in a crafters library,"* says Arts 'N Crafts Showguide. 58 pages.
Item #150 $7.95

Licensing Art and Design *by Caryn Leland*

Whether a designer, illustrator, photographer, or fine artist, you can increase your income by licensing your creative images and this book will show you how. Expert coverage includes explanation of copyright, trademark law, licensing agreements, how to maximize your royalties, a negotiation checklist to help evaluate deals, model agreements for licensing, and how to find manufacturers and distributors. 112 pages.
Item #133 $16.95

The Law *(In Plain English)* for Crafts People *by Leonard DuBoff.* This valuable "Plain English" book helps you prevent the problems that are preventable and cope with the rest. It may save you many times its price in legal fees. Includes information on forms of organization, trademarks, copyrights, contracts, consignment sales, how to keep taxes low, product liability, collections, insurance, how to find a lawyer and more. 148 pages, softcover. Item #134 $12.95

Business Forms and Contracts for Crafts People *by Leonard DuBoff.* Companion to *The Law For Crafts People.* Describes most types of forms and contracts with numerous examples. Also includes a checklist for saving time and money when incorporating, IRS requirements when deducting computers, bartering, donating work, and forms of record. Covers consignment and commission contracts. 110 pages, softcover. Item #135 $14.95

The How-To's of Gift Baskets, *Growing a Successful Gift Basket Business* *by Carol Starr.* Gives a step-by-step process for starting one's own gift basket service. Covers everything for the beginning gift basket entrepreneur: licensing, working from home, in depth marketing strategy, assembling, designing and provides a list of suppliers. A person with limited funds can start out at less than $500 and has the opportunity to gross $50,000 the first year. 150 pages, softcover, illustrated.
Item #111 $14.95

Photographing Your Artwork *by Steve Meltzer*
The Crafts Report photography columnist has produced a book for all craftspeople who ever had the need to hold a camera and shoot their work. Steve shares hundreds of tricks and techniques to make your slides and prints more effective. The book also tells how to get the best buys on new and secondhand equipment, explains indoor and outdoor lighting, and how to insure color retention. Softcover.   Item #139 $12.95

Publishing Your Art as Cards, Posters & Calendars, *A Complete Guide to Creating, Designing, & Marketing by Harold Davis.* A practical manual for artists wishing to publish their work for additional income and enhancing their reputation. Covers finding a publisher, royalties, self-publishing, successful techniques of image creation, market research, finding a printer, managing your business, glossary of technical terms, index, and appendices. 168 pages, softcover, illustrated.
Item #113 $19.95

The Basic Guide to Selling Arts & Crafts
by James Dillehay. Gives step-by-step help on over 150 topics. Find the best fairs, sell to stores, get interior designers and corporations to buy your work, make money from spin-off ideas, sell your crafts mail order, discover overlooked markets, what to do when your work isn't selling. Appendixes list over 250 sources and reference books for the artisan. Selected as the official text of the American Professional Crafter's Guild. 224 pages, softcover, illustrations.
Item #100 $14.95

"The blueprint for success in the crafts industry."
CRAFTMASTER NEWS

"This book will pay for itself many times over if you want to make money with your work."
GLASS CRAFTERS

"A comprehensive, user-friendly text on all aspects of starting and growing a craft business, we highly recommend "Guide to Selling Arts & Crafts."
THE CRAFTS FAIR GUIDE

What if there were a way . . .

. . . FOR YOU TO EARN an income in a proven, professional career:
√ that was affordable to start...
√ that provided you the opportunity to be your own boss...
√ that allowed you to work part-time or full-time -- when, where and the way you chose, with the people you chose to work with...
√ that educated and trained you, too...
√ that was based on a proven, duplicatable system that had already worked for tens of thousands of average people...
√ and where, with a little luck and lots of work, hitting the jackpot was truly possible?

AND WHAT IF THAT CAREER OPPORTUNITY were open to everybody; if your age, sex, education, race, religion, start-up money, past success or failure . . . truly didn't matter at all?

WHAT IF advancement in this profession were based on helping others succeed? What if the more you helped other people achieve in terms of money, advancement and recognition, the more of all of those things you received as well?

And what if $300 to $500 to $1,000 a month part-time, $3,000 to $5,000 and more full-time were truly possible for you...? Would an extra $12,000 a year appeal to you? How about the real possibility of doubling to tripling your present income?

And what if the top income earners in the profession were taking home $10,000, $30,000 a month or more -- some of them, much, *much,* more! Would any of that interest you?

If all that you just read were true, legal and viable, and people just like you were already doing it and succeeding -- would you be willing to take a closer look at it?

Well, all that you've just read *is real and true,* and as millions of people around the world are discovering, Network Marketing Sales may be your ticket to earning the money you want and providing you with the life-style you've always dreamed of, plus a whole lot more! You can learn more about it in . . .

Money, Money, Money, Money, Money

by John Milton Fogg

This 64-page paperback can be read in about half an hour. It's the kind of book you can't put down. It offers an incredible opportunity that could change your life right now! Order your copy today, send $4.95 (includes shipping) to W. Snow Publishers, P.O. Box 75, Torreon, NM 87061. Comes with Risk-free, Money-Back Guarantee.

OVERCOMING THE 7 DEVILS THAT RUIN SUCCESS
by James Dillehay

Everyone is familiar with failure and self-sabotage. After enough of it, some of us even figure out ways to stop ruining our lives and do the things we really want to do. This easy-to-read guide offers exercises for avoiding self-defeating habits, mindless work routines, and self-doubt. Dillehay's own lessons began when a teacher first appeared telling him to leave his prosperous but unfulfilling career. Trading fortune and security to study with a Sufi master, Dillehay encounters seven devils of the ego, i.e., *False Success, Fear, Guilt, Vanity, Impatience, Habit* and *The Clock*. The book also gives exercises anyone can use to identify and follow their dreams to higher achievements. Item #200 $6.95

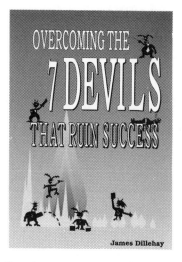

"*Filled with great wisdom*"
The New Times

"*I recommend it highly*"
InnerSelf Magazine

"*Stories of his experiences interweave with exercises for transforming self-defeating habits into a positive ally called 'the intelligence of the heart.'*"
Whole Self Times

CostCutters News
for Your Small Business

CostCutters News is a bimonthly newsletter packed with hundreds of proven ways to reduce all your business expenses. Learn how to reduce travel, insurance, advertising, office supplies, telephone, and hundreds of other expenses. Save time and money. One issue alone gives you enough ideas to save many times over the cost of a subscription, only $19.95 a year. For a sample issue, send $3.50 to: *CostCutters News*, Box 75, Torreon, NM 87061.

Order Form - Copy, Fill Out and Mail Today

Order three or more books, receive a 10% discount. (Only books are discounted, shipping remains the same). Order by credit card, call **800-235-6570** or mail your check or money order today along with a copy of this order form to Craft Business Books, P.O. Box 75, Torreon, NM 87061. Shipping and handling is $3.50 for the first book and $.50 for each additional book within the U.S.. Orders are shipped within 24 hours.

SHIP TO (please print clearly):

Name_____

Address_____

City, State, Zip_____

Phone_____   *Order by phone,*
                                    call 800-235-6570

ITEM #	TITLE	QTY	PRICE	TOTAL

Shipping & handling: add $3.50 for first book and $.50 for each additional book.

For Canada, shipping is $5.00 for first book and $1 for each addtl. Payment in U.S. funds only.

SUBTOTAL	
LESS DISCOUNT	
SHIPPING	
TOTAL	

We guarantee your complete satisfaction. If you are unhappy with any book ordered from this catalog, return it to us in good condition within 60 days for a complete refund. No questions asked.

Index

A

B